Ahead of you stretches your future, like a road leading into the distance. Along that road are ambitions you wish to realize and desires you wish to gratify. To fulfill your ambitions and desires, you must be successful with money. Use the financial principles made clear in the pages that follow. Let them guide you away from the confines of a lean purse to that happier, more fulfilling life a fat purse can bring. Like the law of gravity, the laws of gold are universal and unchanging. May they prove to you, as they have proven to so many others, a sure path to a fat purse, larger bank balances, and gratifying financial progress.

For Nyle

Seek knowledge and you will find all of life's treasures

MONEY IS PLENTIFUL FOR THOSE WHO UNDERSTAND
THE SIMPLE RULES OF ITS ACQUISITION.

1. Start fattening your purse
2. Control your expenses
3. Make your gold multiply
4. Guard your treasures from loss
5. Make your home a profitable investment
6. Insure a future income
7. Increase your ability to earn

The Richest Man in Babylon

Modern Language Edition
Updated by Luke Wilson

Original Text by George S. Clason

Modern Language Press, LLC

ISBN: 979-8-9869315-0-0 (paperback)

ISBN: 979-8-9869315-1-7 (ebook)

Library of Congress Control Number: 2022946282

This book is not intended to be a source of financial or legal advice. Making adjustments to a financial strategy or plan should only be undertaken after consulting with a professional, not a fictional ancient citizen of Babylon. The publisher and the author make no guarantee of financial results obtained by using this book.

Published by Modern Language Press, LLC, Torrance, California USA.

First printing edition 2022

Modern Language Press, LLC

4733 Torrance Blvd #617

Torrance, CA 90503-4100

inquiries@modernlanguagepress.com

www.richestbabylon.com

www.modernlanguagepress.com

Table of Contents

The Man Who
Desired Gold

Bansir, the chariot builder of Babylon, was thoroughly discouraged. From his seat upon the low wall surrounding his property, he gazed sadly at his simple home and the open workshop in which stood a partially completed chariot.

His wife frequently appeared at the open door. Her worried glances in his direction reminded him that the grain meal bag was almost empty, and he should be at work finishing the chariot, hammering and hewing, polishing and painting, stretching the leather taut over the wheel rims, preparing it for delivery, so he could collect from his wealthy client.

Nevertheless, his fat, muscular body sat impassively upon the wall. His mind was struggling patiently with a problem for which he could find no answer.

The hot, tropical sun, so typical of this valley of the Euphrates, beat down upon him mercilessly. Beads of perspiration formed on his brow and trickled down unnoticed to lose themselves in his hairy jungle of a chest.

Beyond his home, the high, terraced wall surrounding the King's palace towered overhead. Nearby, severing the blue sky, was the painted tower of the Temple of Bel. In the shadow of such grandeur was his simple home and many others far less neat and well cared for. Babylon was like this—a mixture of grandeur and squalor, of dazzling wealth and dire poverty, crowded together without plan or system, within the protecting walls of the city.

He would have seen behind him, had he cared to turn and look, the noisy chariots of the rich as they jostled and crowded aside the sandaled tradesmen as well as the barefooted beggars. Even the rich were forced to turn into the gutters to clear the way for the long lines of slaves carrying water, on "the King's Business," each transporting a heavy goatskin of water to be poured upon the hanging gardens.

Bansir was too engrossed in his own problem to hear or heed the confused hubbub of the busy city. It was the unexpected twanging of the strings from a familiar guitar that aroused him from his thoughts. He turned and looked into the sensitive, smiling face of his best friend—Kobbi, the musician.

"I wish you prosperity, my good friend," began Kobbi with an elaborate salute. "But it looks like you have more than enough—you won't have to work a day in your life! I am really happy for you, and if I were in your position, I'd share my good fortune with you. Could you please lend me two pieces of copper for the nobleman's feast tonight? I know you have enough to share with me. I'll return them as soon as I'm finished and you won't even know they are gone."

"If I had two pieces of copper," Bansir responded gloomily, "I wouldn't be able to share them, not even with you, my best friend. Those two pieces of copper would be all I have, and nobody gives away all of their money—not even to their best friend."

"What?" exclaimed Kobbi with genuine surprise, "You don't have a single piece of copper, but here you are sitting like a statue up on this wall! Why don't you work on that chariot? How else will you be able to pay for your expensive tastes? This is not like you, my friend. Where is your endless energy? Is something bothering you?"

"I guess the gods are tormenting me," Bansir said. "It began with a dream, a senseless dream, in which I thought I was rich. I had a nice bag hanging from my belt that was full of coins that I tossed carelessly to beggars. There were pieces of silver I used to buy whatever my wife or I wanted, and I had enough gold saved for my future that I was happy and free of worries. You wouldn't have recognized me as your hardworking friend. My wife didn't recognize me in the dream, as her face was glowing like it once did when we first married."

"That does sound like a nice dream," commented Kobbi, "but why would this lead you to act like a statue on a wall?"

"Because, when I woke up and remembered how little money I had, a feeling of rebellion came over me. Can I talk about it with you? You know, since we had the same upbringing and have known each other for so long. When we were boys, we went to the priests to ask for their guidance; as young men, we shared the same interests and pleasures; as grown men, we are close friends and content with our lives. We've been fine working long hours and spending our earnings freely. We have earned so much money over the last several years, but we can only dream about the joys that come from wealth. Ugh! Are we anything more than just dumb sheep? We live in the richest city in the world—travelers say no other city compares.

"There is so much wealth around us and we have none of it. After half a lifetime of working hard, you, my best friend, have no money and say to me, 'May I borrow such an insignificant amount of money as two pieces of copper until after the nobleman's feast tonight?' Then, what do I say? Do I say, 'Here is my purse; my money is yours.' No, I admit that my purse is as empty as yours. What's the matter? Why can't we acquire an abundance of silver and gold so we can buy more than just the bare necessities?

"And think about our sons," Bansir continued, "aren't they following in our footsteps? Should our sons and their families have to live all their lives surrounded by wealth that they can't have, and be content to survive on sour goat's milk and porridge?"

"I've never heard you speak to me like this, Bansir." Kobbi was puzzled.

"Well, I've never thought like this before. From dawn to dusk, I have worked to build the finest chariots anybody could make, half-heartedly hoping one day the gods would recognize my work ethic and reward me—this of course has yet to happen and I know it never will. This is saddening because I wish I was a rich man. I wish I had land and cattle, fine clothes and coins in my purse. I am willing to work hard for these things with all my strength, skill, and mental capacity, but I wish I was fairly compensated. What is the matter with us? Tell me, why can't we have our equal share of our city's prosperity?"

"I wish I had the answer!" Kobbi replied. "I'm no more satisfied than you. The money I earn playing my guitar is spent quickly. I dream that the money I earn would be enough for my family to not go hungry. I wish I had a guitar grand enough that it could truly sing the strains of music that surge through my mind. With that kind of instrument, I could make music unlike anything even the King has heard before."

"You should have a guitar like that! Nobody in Babylon can play as well as you; not only the King, but the gods themselves would be delighted. But how would you get such an instrument while we both are as poor as the King's slaves?"

"Listen to the bell! Here they come."

He pointed to the long column of half-naked, sweating water bearers plodding laboriously up the narrow street from the river. They marched in rows of five, each bent under a heavy goatskin of water.

"He is a good man, their leader." Kobbi indicated the wearer of the bell who marched in front without a load. "He was clearly a prominent man in his own country."

"There are many good people in the line," Bansir agreed, "as good as we are. People from the far North and South, and people from countries near ours. All marching together from the river to the gardens, back and forth, day after day, year after year. No happiness to look forward to. They must sleep on straw and eat hard grain porridge. Pity those poor people, Kobbi!"

"I do pity them, but you've made me see that we are barely better off than them, even though we are free men."

"That's the truth, Kobbi, unpleasant as it may be. We don't want to go on year after year living slavish lives. Working, working, working and getting nowhere!"

"Can't we find out how others get rich and live lavish lives?" Kobbi inquired.

"Maybe there is some secret we can learn if we ask people," replied Bansir thoughtfully.

"Today," suggested Kobbi, "I saw our old friend, Arkad, riding in his golden chariot. But he didn't look over my humble head as many in his position would have done. Instead, he waved at me so that all onlookers would see him greeting Kobbi, the musician."

"Apparently, he is the richest man in Babylon," Bansir mused.

"He is so rich that the King is rumored to ask his advice regarding the treasury," Kobbi replied.

"So rich," Bansir added, "I'm afraid that if I saw him in the middle of the night, I would have to steal his fat purse."

"Nonsense," reproved Kobbi, "one's wealth is not in the purse one carries. A fat purse empties quickly if there is no income to refill it. Arkad has an income that constantly keeps his purse full, no matter how liberally he spends."

"Income, that is the thing," exclaimed Bansir. "I wish I had an income that would keep flowing into my purse whether I sat on the wall or traveled to far lands. I'm sure Arkad can recommend a way we can make an income. Do you think he could explain it in simple terms to me?"

"Probably—I think he passed his knowledge to his son, Nomasir," Kobbi responded.

"I've heard rumors that Nomasir went to Nineveh and became, without his father's help, one of the richest men in that city."

"Kobbi, you bring a curious thought to mind." A new light gleamed in Bansir's eyes. "It costs nothing to ask wise advice from a good friend and Arkad was always that. It doesn't matter how empty our purses are—that shouldn't have to hold us back. We are tired of being poor men in a rich city—we want to be rich men. Let's go ask Arkad how we can develop incomes for ourselves."

"You inspire me, Bansir. You challenge me to think in ways I've never thought before. You've made me realize the reason why we have never been rich—we never sought it. You have worked patiently to build the strongest chariots in Babylon. You devoted most of your energy to your work and you succeeded at it. In my case, I strove to become a skillful guitar player, at which I succeeded as well. We succeeded in areas in our life that we devoted the most time and energy toward.

"The gods were okay to let us continue living this way. Now, at last, we see a light as bright as the rising sun. The light invites us to learn more so that we can prosper. With a new understanding we can find honest ways to fulfill our desires."

"Let's go see Arkad today," Bansir urged, "Also, we should ask our poor childhood friends to join us so that they can learn from Arkad as well."

"You've always been my most thoughtful friend, Bansir. That's why you have so many friends. I agree that we should go to our friends and invite them to come with us today."

The Richest Man
In Babylon

In old Babylon, there once lived a very rich man named Arkad. Far and wide he was famed for his great wealth and generosity; he was generous in his charities, he was generous with his family, and he was liberal in his own expenses. Nevertheless, each year his wealth increased more rapidly than he spent it.

Some friends from younger days came to him and said: "You're more fortunate than we are, Arkad. You have become the richest man in Babylon while we struggle to survive. You can wear the finest clothes and enjoy the rarest foods, while we have to settle for giving our families the simplest clothes and feeding them as best we can.

"Yet, we were once equal. We went to the same schools and played the same games. You didn't outshine us in our studies or the games. In the years since, you haven't been any more of an honorable citizen than we have.

"As far as we can see, you haven't worked harder or more faithfully than us, and you do not appear to have any superior powers or wisdom. Why, then, should random fate allow you to enjoy all the good things in life and ignore us who are equally deserving?"

Thereupon Arkad scolded them, "If, in your whole life, you haven't been able to make more money than you need just to survive, it is because you either have failed to learn the laws that govern the building of wealth, or simply don't follow the laws.

"Random fate is a vicious goddess who brings no permanent good to anyone. She will eventually ruin the lives of everyone who was given more money than they needed. She produces people with overzealous spending habits, who soon spend all they have and are left with overwhelming appetites and desires they can't gratify. Others will hoard their wealth, afraid to spend what they have, knowing they wouldn't be able to replace it. They are plagued with fears of robbers and doom themselves to lives of emptiness and secret misery.

"There are of course others who can take unearned money, add to it, and continue to be happy and contented citizens, but there are so few of them. Think of the people you know who have inherited wealth suddenly, and see if these patterns hold true."

His friends admitted that of the people they knew who had inherited wealth these words were true, and they asked him to explain to them how he became so wealthy, so he continued: "As a young man, I looked around me and saw all the good things there were that bring happiness and contentment, and realized that wealth increased the benefits of all these. Wealth is a power. With wealth many things are possible.

"One might decorate a home with expensive furnishings. One might sail the distant seas. One might feast on the fine foods of far away lands. One might buy expensive items made of gold and stone. One might even build mighty temples for the gods. One might do all these things and many others that delight the senses and gratify the soul.

"When I realized all this, I decided that I would claim my share of the good things of life. I would not be one of those people who stands in the shadows, enviously watching others enjoy their riches. I wouldn't settle for wearing cheap clothes and I wouldn't be satisfied with the life of a poor man. On the contrary, I would make myself a guest at this banquet of good things.

"As the son of a humble merchant, being part of a large family with no hope of an inheritance, and not having any, as you have so frankly said, superior powers or wisdom, I decided that if I was going to get what I wanted, time and studying would be required.

"As for time, everyone has it in abundance. Each of you have let precious time, during which you could have acquired wealth, slip by. Yet, you admit you have nothing to show except your good families, of which you have a right to be proud.

"As for study, remember that our wise teacher showed us there are two kinds of learning: one is what we are taught and know, the other is the training that allows us to discover that which we did not know. So, I learned how to accumulate wealth, and I made this my task and did it well.

"I found a job as a scribe in the hall of records, and I spent long hours every day carving on the clay tablets. Week after week, and month after month, I worked hard, earning little money. Food, clothing, and offerings to the gods absorbed all my earnings. But my determination did not leave me.

"And one day, Algamish, the moneylender, came to the house of the city master to order a copy of the Ninth Law, and he said to me, 'if you can get this done in two days, I'll give you two coppers.'

"So I worked hard, but the Ninth Law took a long time to copy, and when Algamish returned, I was not finished yet. He was angry, and if I had been his slave, he would have beaten me. But knowing the city master would not let him injure me, I was not scared, so I said to him, 'Algamish, you are a very rich man. Tell me how I can also become rich, and all night I will work on your copy of the Ninth Law, so that it will be finished by morning.'

"He smiled at me and replied, 'You sure are a direct bastard, but let's call it a deal.'

"All that night I worked on his copy until my back and head hurt and I could hardly see. When he returned in the morning, the copies were complete.

"'Now,' I said, 'tell me what you promised.'

"'You have fulfilled your part of our bargain, my son,' he said to me kindly, 'and I am ready to fulfill mine. I will tell you what you want to know because I am getting old, and old men love to talk. When young people come to old people for advice, the young person receives years of wisdom. Young people often think that old people only hold wisdom of the past which wouldn't apply to the modern day. But remember this, the sun that shines today is the same sun that shone when your parents were born, and will still be shining when your last grandchild passes into the darkness.

"'The thoughts of young people,' he continued, 'are bright lights that shine like shooting stars illuminating the night sky, but the wisdom of old people is like the fixed stars that shine so unchangingly that the sailor depends on them to know which way to go. Listen closely because if you don't, you won't be able to grasp the truth that I'll tell you, and you will think that your work last night was for nothing.'

"Then he looked at me wisely from under his shaggy brows and said in a low, forceful tone: 'I found the road to wealth when I decided that a part of all I earned was mine to keep. And so will you.'

"Then he continued to look at me piercingly, but said no more.

"'Is that all?' I asked.

"'That was enough to change a sheep herder into a moneylender,' he replied.

"'But all I earn *is* mine to keep, isn't it?' I demanded.

"'Far from it,' he replied. 'Don't you pay for your clothes and shoes? Don't you pay for your food? Can you live in Babylon without spending? What do you have to show for your earnings of the past month? What about the past year? Fool! You pay everyone but yourself and you work for others, you fool. You may as well be a slave and work for what your master gives you to eat and wear. If you saved one-tenth of your earnings each time you were paid, how much would you have in ten years?'

"Being good at math I answered, 'As much as I earn in one year.'

"'Not quite,' he retorted. 'Every bit of money you save is a slave to work for you. Every bit of money your savings earns is its child who also can work for you. If you become wealthy, then your savings will earn money, and that can pay for the extravagant lifestyle you want.

"'You think I scammed you for your long night's work,' he continued, 'but I am paying you a thousand times over if you have the intelligence to grasp the truth I offer you. A part of all you earn is yours to keep. It should not be less than a tenth, no matter how little you earn. Save even more if you can afford it. Pay yourself first.

"'Wealth, like a tree, grows from a tiny seed. The first piece of copper you save is the seed from which your tree of wealth shall grow. The sooner you plant that seed the sooner the tree will grow. And the more faithfully you nourish and water that tree with consistent savings, the sooner you can enjoy the easy life of wealth.'

"After this, he took the copies I made for him and went away.

"I thought a lot about what he said to me, and it seemed reasonable, so I decided that I would try it. Each time I was paid, I took one out of the ten pieces of copper I earned and hid it away. And strange as it may seem, I didn't feel the money's absence when I went about my daily life with nine pieces of copper instead of ten. I was often tempted as my savings grew to spend it on some of the fine goods the merchants were selling, brought by camels and ships from the land of the Phoenicians. But I was able to hold myself back.

"A year after Algamish left, he came back and said to me, 'Son, have you saved at least one-tenth of all you have earned this last year?'

"I answered proudly, 'Yes, master, I have.'

"'That is good,' he answered beaming at me, 'and what have you done with it?'

"'I gave it to Azmur, the brickmaker, who told me he was traveling over to Tyre and would buy me some rare jewels from the Phoenicians. When he comes back we will sell the jewels at high prices and divide the earnings.'

"'Every fool must learn,' he growled, 'but why trust the knowledge of a brickmaker about jewels? Would you go to the baker to inquire about the stars? No, you would go to the astronomer, if you thought for one minute. Your savings are gone, kid, you have yanked your wealth-tree up by the roots. Plant another, try again. And next time if you would like advice about jewels, go to the jewel merchant. If you want to learn about sheep, go to the shepherd. Advice is one thing that is freely given away, but make sure you take only what is worth having. Those who take advice about their savings from one who is inexperienced will lose their savings, proving the inaccuracy of the advice.' After saying this, he went away.

"And Algamish was right. The Phoenicians were scoundrels and sold Azmur worthless bits of glass that looked like gems. But as Algamish had instructed me, I again saved one out of ten pieces of copper; I had formed the habit and it was no longer difficult.

"Again, one year later, Algamish came to the room of records I worked at and addressed me.

"'What progress have you made since the last time I saw you?'

"'I have made a good habit of saving,' I replied, 'and I entrusted my savings to Agger, the shield maker, to buy bronze, and every four months he pays me interest.'

"'That is good. And what do you do with the interest you earned?'

"'I have a great feast with honey, fine wine, and spiced cake. I have also bought myself a scarlet shirt. And someday I will buy myself a donkey to ride.'

"Algamish laughed, 'You eat the children of your savings! How do you expect them to work for you, and how can they have children that will also work for you? How do you expect your money to grow? First earn interest from your savings, and then you can enjoy numerous banquets without regret.' He went away again.

"I didn't see him again for two years; when he returned, his face was full of deep lines and his eyes drooped, as he was becoming a very old man. He said to me, 'Arkad, have you achieved the wealth you dreamed of?'

"And I answered, 'Not quite, but I have some savings and it continues to earn more, and its earnings earn more.'

"'And do you still take the advice of brickmakers?'

"'Well, they give good advice about brickmaking,' I retorted.

"'Arkad,' he continued, 'you have learned your lessons well. First, you learned to live on less than you earned. Next, you learned to seek advice from those who are experts in their own fields. Lastly, you have learned to make your money work for you.

"'You have taught yourself how to earn money, how to keep it, and how to use it. You have proven to be trustworthy and responsible. I am becoming an old man. My sons only think of spending money and give no thought to earning. My wealth is great and I'm afraid it will become too much for me to look after. If you go to Nippur and look after my land there, I will make you my partner and you will hold a share of my estate.'

"So I went to Nippur and took charge of his holdings, which were large. And because I was full of ambition and because I had mastered the three laws of successfully handling wealth that Algamish had taught me, I was able to greatly increase the value of his properties.

"When Algamish died, I received his estate," said Arkad, and when he had finished his tale, one of his friends said, "You were lucky that Algamish made you an heir."

"Lucky only in a sense that I had the desire to be rich before I met him. For four years I proved my perseverance by keeping one-tenth of all I earned. Would you call a fisherman lucky who studied the habits of the fish for years so that when the wind changed, he could still catch plentiful fish? Opportunity is an arrogant goddess who wastes no time with people who are unprepared."

"You had strong willpower to keep on trying after you lost your first year's savings. You are unusual in that way," spoke up another.

"Willpower!" retorted Arkad. "What nonsense. Do you think willpower gives a person the strength to lift something so heavy that not even a camel could carry it, or to lead stubborn cattle who refuse to move? Willpower is the unflinching purpose to finish a task completely. If I set a goal for myself, no matter how difficult and tedious, I will finish it. How else would I have confidence in myself to do more important things? If I said to myself, 'for a hundred days when I walk across the bridge into the city, I will pick a pebble up from the road and throw it into the stream,' I would do it.

"If on the seventh day I passed by without remembering, I would not say to myself, 'tomorrow I will throw two pebbles and it will be like I didn't even forget to do so today.' Instead, I would go back and throw the pebble before continuing on my way. Nor on the twentieth day would I say to myself, 'Arkad, this is useless. What good does throwing a pebble every day do? Throw in a handful and be done with it.' No, I would not say or do it. When I set a goal for myself, I complete it. So I am careful not to start difficult and impractical tasks, because I value my free time."

Then another friend spoke up and said, "If what you say is true, that this is such a simple task, why doesn't everyone do it? And wouldn't there be a shortage of wealth?"

"Wealth grows wherever one exerts energy," Arkad replied. "If a rich person builds a new palace, is the money they paid to have it built gone? No, the brickmaker has part of it, the laborer has part of it, and the architect has part of it. Yet when the palace was completed, wasn't it worth the money? And isn't the land the palace is on worth more now? And isn't the land of nearby properties worth more because of the new palace? Wealth grows in magic ways. No one can predict its limit. Haven't the Phoenicians built great cities on barren coasts with the wealth that comes from their ships of commerce on the seas?"

"What do you think we should do to become rich?" asked another friend. "The years have passed and we are no longer young men who have money to save."

"I recommend that you listen to the wisdom of Algamish and say to yourselves, 'A part of all I earn is mine to keep.' Say it in the morning when you first wake up. Say it at noon. Say it at night. Say it each hour of every day. Say it to yourself until the words stand out like letters of fire across the sky. Impress yourself with the idea and fill yourself with the thought. Then take whatever portion seems wise, as long as it is more than one-tenth, and store it away. Soon you will realize what a rich feeling it is to own a treasure that only you are entitled to. As it grows it will stimulate you. A new joy of life will thrill you, and you will begin to exert greater efforts to earn more. As you earn more, the same percentage would be yours to keep. Then learn to make your money work for you—make it your slave. Make its children and its children's children work for you.

"Ensure an income for your future. Look at the elderly and remember that you will one day be in their shoes. Invest your money with caution so that it is not lost. Unfair rates of return are like bait on a hook to catch a fish and reel it in toward its death.

"It is important to save small amounts at regular intervals so that your family will not starve if you die suddenly. The prudent person does not delay saving for their family's future needs in expectation of a windfall.

"Befriend wise people and seek the advice of people whose daily work is handling money. Let them save you from making the same mistake that I made in entrusting my money to Azmur, the brickmaker. A small return and a safe investment is much more desirable than risk.

"Enjoy life while you can. Do not overstrain or try to save too much. If one-tenth of all you earn is as much as you can comfortably keep, be content to keep this portion. Live otherwise according to your income and do not let not yourself get too frugal and afraid to spend. Life is good and life is rich with worthwhile things to enjoy."

His friends thanked him and went away. Some were silent because they had no imagination and could not understand. Some were sarcastic because they thought that someone so rich should share his money with old friends who are less fortunate. But some took a lot from Arkad's story and saw money in a new light. They realized that Algamish had come back to the room of the scribes because he was watching Arkad work his way out of darkness into light. When Arkad found the light, a place awaited him. He could not fill that place until he had worked out his own understanding, until he was ready for the opportunity.

In the following years, these latter people frequently visited Arkad, who received his friends gladly. He talked with them and gave them more advice, as people with a lot of experience are often glad to do. And he assisted them in investing their savings so that it would earn good interest safely, and would neither be lost nor entangled in investments that paid no dividends.

The turning point in these peoples' lives came the day they realized the truth that had come from Algamish to Arkad and from Arkad to them.

A PART OF ALL YOU EARN IS YOURS TO KEEP.

Seven Cures For
a Lean Purse

The glory of Babylon endures. Down through the ages its reputation comes to us as the richest of cities, with treasures most fabulous. But it was not always like this. The riches of Babylon were the results of the wisdom of its people. They first had to learn how to become wealthy.

When the Good King, Sargon, returned to Babylon after defeating his enemies, the Elamites, he was confronted with a serious situation. The Royal Chancellor explained it to the King:

"Ever since your majesty ordered construction of the great irrigation canals and the mighty temples of the gods, our people have seen many prosperous years. Now that these works are completed, our people seem unable to support themselves. The laborers are unemployed, the merchants have few customers, and the farmers are unable to sell their produce. The people don't have enough money to buy food."

"But where has all the money gone that we spent for these improvements?" demanded the King.

"I'm afraid it has found its way into the possession of a few very rich people in our city," responded the Chancellor. "The money fell through the fingers of most of our people as quickly as milk goes through a strainer. Now that the stream of money has stopped flowing, most of our people have no way to earn any more."

The King was thoughtful for some time, then he asked, "Why should so few people be able to acquire all the money?"

"Because they know how," replied the Chancellor. "We shouldn't condemn someone for succeeding because they know how. We shouldn't take away the money a rich person has earned to give to the poorer people who have less ability."

"But why," demanded the King, "shouldn't everyone learn how to earn a lot of money and become rich and prosperous?"

"Quite possible, your excellency. But who can teach them? Definitely not the priests, because they don't know how to make money."

"Who in our city knows the most about how to become wealthy, Chancellor?" asked the King.

"Your question answers itself, your majesty. Who is the richest man in Babylon?"

"Well said, my able Chancellor. It is Arkad. He is the richest man in Babylon. Bring him here tomorrow."

The next day, as the King had commanded, Arkad appeared before him, straight and sprightly despite being 70 years old.

"Arkad," spoke the King, "is it true you are the richest man in Babylon?"

"So they say, your majesty, and nobody disputes it."

"How did you become so wealthy?"

"By taking advantage of opportunities available to all citizens of our good city."

"You had nothing to start with?"

"Besides having a great desire for wealth, no."

"Arkad," continued the King, "our city is in a depressed state because a few people know how to acquire wealth, therefore monopolizing it, while most of our citizens don't know how to keep any of the money they earn.

"I want Babylon to be the wealthiest city in the world. In order for this to happen, it must be a city of many wealthy people. So, we should teach everyone how to get rich. Tell me, Arkad, is there any secret to getting rich? Can it be taught?"

"It is practical, your majesty. What I know can be taught to others."

The King's eyes glowed. "Arkad, that is exactly what I wanted to hear. Can you be the leader of this endeavor? Can you share your knowledge with a school for teachers, so that they can teach others until everybody in my domain has your knowledge?"

Arkad bowed and said, "I would be honored. I will gladly share my knowledge to better my community and glorify my King. Have your Chancellor arrange a class for me to teach one hundred students and I will share the seven cures I used to fatten my purse, which was the skinniest in Babylon before I acquired my riches."

Two weeks later, in compliance with the King's command, the one hundred students chosen by the King assembled in the great hall in the Temple of Learning, lounging on colorful rugs in a semicircle. Arkad sat beside a small table upon which sat a sacred lamp emitting a smoke with a strange and pleasing odor.

"This is the richest man in Babylon," whispered a student, nudging his neighbor as Arkad arose. "He is only a man, just like the rest of us."

"As a faithful subject of our great King," Arkad began, "I stand before you per his request. Because I was once a poor young man who wanted to be rich, and because I found knowledge that enabled me to acquire riches, the King asks that I share my knowledge with you.

"I acquired my riches humbly. I was in the same position as you and every citizen in Babylon—I had no advantages. I hated the emptiness of my purse; I wanted it to be round and full, clinking with the sound of gold. So, I looked for a way to fatten my lean purse—I found seven. I will explain to you all seven cures for a lean purse, which I recommend to everyone who desires riches. Every day, for seven days, I will share one of the seven remedies with you.

"Listen closely to what I'm about to share with you. Debate it with me. Discuss it among yourselves. Learn these lessons thoroughly, so that you too may attain wealth. First, each of you must start earning money. Only then will you be competent, and be able to teach these truths to others.

"I will teach you simple ways to fatten your purses. This is the first step toward the temple of wealth, and no one can continue until they plant their feet firmly upon the first step. Let's consider the first cure."

The First Cure: Start fattening your purse

Arkad addressed a thoughtful man in the second row. "My good friend, what do you do for a living?"

"I am a scribe who carves records on clay tablets," replied the man.

"That's what I did when I was first earning money. So, you have the same opportunity to build a fortune."

He spoke to a rosy-cheeked man, farther back. "And tell me, what do you do for a living?"

"I am a meat butcher," responded this man. "I buy the goats raised by the farmers, kill them, and sell the meat to housewives and the skins to sandal makers."

"Because you also labor and earn, you have every advantage to succeed that I had."

In this way did Arkad proceed to find out how each person labored to earn their living. When he was finished questioning them, he said:

"Now, my students, you can see that there are many ways to earn money. Whichever way you earn your money is a stream of money from which you can divert your labors into your purse. Therefore, into each of your purses flows a stream of coins large or small according to your ability. Does that make sense?"

They nodded and murmured in agreement. "Then," continued Arkad, "if each of you wish to build a fortune, shouldn't you start by utilizing the source of wealth that has already been established?" To this they agreed.

Then Arkad turned to a humble man who had declared himself an egg merchant. "If you select one of your baskets and put ten eggs into it each morning and take nine eggs out each evening, what will eventually happen?"

"It will overflow."

"Why?"

"Because each day I put in one more egg than I take out."

Arkad turned to the class with a smile. "Does anyone here have a lean purse?"

They looked amused, laughing and waving their purses in jest.

"Alright," he continued, "Now I'll tell you the first remedy I learned to cure a lean purse. Do exactly as I have suggested to the egg merchant. For every ten coins you place in your purse use only nine. Your purse will start to fatten immediately and its increasing weight will feel good in your hands and bring satisfaction to your soul.

"Don't ignore what I said because it is simple—truth is always simple. I said I would tell you how I built my fortune—this was my beginning. I, too, carried a lean purse and cursed it because there was nothing in it to satisfy my desires. But when I began to take only nine of the ten coins I put in, it began to fatten. So will yours.

"Now let me tell you something that I cannot explain. When I spent no more than ninety percent of my income, I didn't notice the absence of the other ten percent. I did not feel poorer than before. Before long, coins came to me more easily than before. It must be a law of the gods that those who save and do not spend will earn money more easily. Likewise, those who have an empty purse repel money.

"What do you want the most? Is it the gratification of your daily wants: a jewel, decorations for your home, clothes, things that are quickly gone and forgotten about? Or is it more meaningful belongings such as gold, land, cattle, and income-bringing investments? The coins you take from your purse bring the former. The coins you leave in the purse will bring the latter.

"This, my students, was the first cure I discovered for my lean purse: For each ten coins I put in, I spent only nine. Discuss this amongst yourselves. If any of you proves it untrue, tell me tomorrow when we meet again."

The Second Cure: Control your expenditures

"Some of you have asked me this: How can I save one-tenth of my earnings when not even my entire paycheck is enough to sustain me?" Arkad addressed his students on the second day. "Yesterday, how many of you carried lean purses?"

"All of us," answered the class.

"Yet, you do not all earn the same—some earn much more than others, and some have much larger families to support. Yet, all purses were equally lean. Let me tell you something weird about people; what each of us call our 'necessary expenses' will naturally grow as our incomes grow so that the proportion remains the same.

"Don't confuse your necessary expenses with desires. Each of you and your families want more than you can afford. So you will spend your money to gratify these desires until the money runs out. You will still, however, have many ungratified desires.

"Everyone is burdened with more desires than they can gratify. Because of my wealth, do you all think that I am able to buy everything I want? This is untrue. There are limits to my time, strength, distances I might travel, what I might eat, and zest with which I can enjoy my life.

"Just like weeds grow in a field wherever the farmer leaves space for their roots, desires will grow freely in people whenever there is a possibility of their being gratified. We have a multitude of desires and are only able to gratify a few.

"Look closely at your accustomed habits of living. Here you will find some expenses that can be reduced or eliminated. Demand of yourself one hundred percent of appreciated value for each coin you spend.

Write down each thing you would like to spend your money on. Circle those that are necessary, and then circle your wants that you can afford with the remaining nine-tenths of your income. Cross out the rest and come to terms with the fact that these desires, like many others, will go ungratified, and that this is okay.

"Then budget your necessary expenses. Do not touch the one-tenth that is fattening your purse. Let this be your great desire that is being fulfilled. Keep working with your budget, and keep adjusting it to help you. Make your budget your first assistant in defending your growing fortune."

Hereupon one of the students, wearing red and gold clothing, arose and said, "I am a free man. I believe that it is my right to enjoy the good things in life. Therefore, I do not like the idea of a budget, because it makes me feel like a slave that is being told how much I can spend and what I can buy. I feel like a budget would take a lot of pleasure from my life and make me little more than a donkey used to carry a burden."

To him Arkad replied, "Who, my friend, would determine your budget?"

"I would," responded the protesting one.

"In that case, if a donkey were to budget his burden, would he include jewels, rugs, and heavy bars of gold? Of course not. He would include hay, grain, and water to keep himself alive on the desert trail.

"The purpose of a budget is to help you grow your savings. It is meant to help you afford your needs and, to an extent, your wants. It will help you realize your most cherished desires by defending them from your casual wishes. Your budget patches up the leaks in your purse and enables you to redirect your spending for more gratifying purchases.

"To conclude, this is the second cure for a lean purse: Budget your expenses so that you will have the money to pay for your needs and wants, and to gratify your worthwhile self-selected desires without spending more than nine-tenths of your earnings."

The Third Cure: Make your gold multiply

"Look at how your lean purse is fattening. You have disciplined yourself to save one-tenth of your earnings. You have controlled your spending to protect your growing savings. Next, we will discuss how to grow your savings. Money in a purse is gratifying to own and satisfies a miserable soul, but it earns nothing. The money you save from your earnings is just the start. The earnings your savings make will build your fortunes." Arkad said on the third day to his class.

"How can we put our money to work? My first investment didn't work out—I lost all of my money. I'll talk more about this later. My first profitable investment was a loan I made to a man named Aggar, a shield maker. Once a year he bought large shipments of bronze from across the sea to use to make shields. Lacking the money he needed to pay the merchants, Aggar would borrow from those who had extra money. He was an honorable man; he would always repay his loans and would pay a liberal interest as he sold his shields. Each time I loaned money to him I also loaned back the interest he paid me. Therefore, not only did my capital increase, but its earnings increased as well. It was so gratifying to have this money returned to my purse.

"Students, one's wealth is not in the coins one carries in their purse; it is the income one builds, the stream of gold that continually flows into their purse and keeps it growing. That is what everyone desires: a steady income whether they are working or not.

"I have acquired a lot of income—so much that I have been called a very rich man. My loans to Aggar were my first training in profitable investment. Gaining wisdom from this experience, I extended my loans and investments as my capital increased. At first, my capital came from just a few sources, but grew to come from many sources later, and I had more and more wealth available for any wise use I may choose.

"From my humble wages I made a great deal of interest, which I used as my golden slaves, each piece of gold working to earn more. As they worked for me, their children worked, and their children's children until the income from their combined efforts grew immense. Money grows quickly when you make reasonable earnings, as you will learn from the following story:

"A farmer, when his first son was born, took ten pieces of silver to a moneylender and asked him to keep it for his son until he turned twenty. The moneylender took the money and said the money will earn one-fourth of its value every four years. The farmer asked for the interest to be added to the principal.

"When the boy turned twenty, the farmer went to the moneylender to inquire about the silver. The moneylender explained that because this sum had been increased by compound interest, the original ten pieces of silver had now grown to thirty and a half pieces.

"The farmer was pleased and, because the son did not need the coins, he left them with the moneylender. When the son turned fifty, the moneylender paid the son one hundred and sixty-seven pieces of silver. In fifty years the investment multiplied itself almost seventeen times.

"This, then, is the third cure for a lean purse: Put each coin to work so that it will reproduce and bring you income, a stream of wealth that will flow constantly into your purse."

The Fourth Cure: Guard your treasures from loss

"Misfortune is attracted to shiny objects. Gold in one's purse must be strongly guarded, or it will be lost. It is wise to secure small amounts of money and learn to protect them before the gods entrust us with larger amounts." Said Arkad to his class on the fourth day.

"Every owner of gold is tempted by investment opportunities where it may seem like they could make a lot of money easily. People will often eagerly enter such investments and urge their family and friends to follow.

"The first principle of investment is security for your original investment, or principal. Is it wise to be intrigued by larger earnings when your principal may be lost? I don't think so. The penalty of risk is probable loss. Study carefully before parting with your money and make sure you will get it back. Do not be misled by your own desires to get rich quick. Before you loan your money to anyone, make sure you know they will repay you, so that you won't unwittingly be giving them your hard-earned money. Before you trust your money to an investment, understand the dangers.

"My own first investment was a tragedy to me at the time. I entrusted an entire year's savings to a brick maker named Azmur who was traveling over the far seas. He agreed to buy rare jewels from the Phoenicians for me when he was in Tyre, which we would then sell and share the profits. The Phoenicians were scoundrels and sold him bits of glass. My money was lost. I now know how unwise it was to entrust a brickmaker to buy rare jewels.

"I speak from experience when I share this advice with you: do not be too confident in your own wisdom when entrusting your money to the possible pitfalls of investments. It is much wiser to consult with those who have experience handling money for profit. This advice will prove to be extremely valuable, as it can save you from losing money.

"This, then, is the fourth cure for a lean purse, and is very important, as it prevents your purse from being emptied once it has been filled: Guard your treasure from loss by investing only where your principal is safe, where you can reclaim it if you want, and where you will not fail to collect a fair interest. Talk with wise people. Seek the advice of those experienced in handling money for profit; let their wisdom protect your treasure from unsafe investments."

The Fifth Cure: Make your home a profitable investment

"If one sets aside nine-tenths of their income to live on, and turns some of this money into a profitable investment without detriment to their well being, then their wealth will grow even faster." Said Arkad to his class at their fifth lesson.

"Too many people of Babylon raise their families in low quality housing. They pay their greedy landlords high rents for rooms where the wives can't tend a garden and the children don't have a place to play their games except in the unclean alleys. No family can fully enjoy life unless they have a plot of ground where children can play and the wife can grow a garden to feed her family. It brings joy to eat the figs from your own trees and the grapes from your own vines. To own a home and to have pride in it puts confidence in one's heart, leading to putting forth greater efforts in other endeavors. So, I recommend that everyone owns the roof over their heads.

"Owning a home is not out of the realm of possibility for any well-intentioned person. Our great King has expanded the walls of Babylon so much that a lot of land is now unused and can be purchased at reasonable prices. Moneylenders readily give money to people who wish to buy homes or land for their families. If you can show that you have contributed a reasonable portion of the necessary funding to pay brick makers and builders, moneylenders will look at you favorably.

"When the house is built, you can pay back the moneylender with the same regularity as you paid your landlord before you owned a home. Since each payment you make will reduce your debt to the moneylender, after a few years, you will not have to pay for your housing at all. At that point, your financial worries will be gone because you are the owner of a valuable property and your only big expense will be the King's taxes.

"There are countless benefits you can receive when you own your own house. It will greatly reduce your cost of living and make more of your earnings available for pleasure spending. This is the fifth cure for a lean purse: Own your own home."

The Sixth Cure: Insure a future income

Arkad addressed his class on the sixth day:

"The life of everyone proceeds from childhood to old age. This is the path of life and nobody can deviate from it unless they die young. It behooves you to arrange an adequate income, and to make preparations for your family if you are no longer able to support them, whether due to loss of youth or loss of life. This lesson will teach you how to prepare a full purse to set aside for the future and for emergencies.

"The wealthy person should give thought to their future. They should plan investments or provisions that will continue to grow safely for years, but are available for withdrawal if needed.

"There are many ways someone can save for their future. They might bury a treasure in a secret hiding spot. But, no matter how well the treasure is hidden, it is still very possible it will get stolen. For this reason, I do not recommend this plan.

"Someone may buy houses or land to save for their future. If the future value of the home or land is considered and real estate is purchased wisely, it is permanent in its value and its value will only increase, providing an abundance of money for the future.

"Someone might give a bit of money for the moneylender to hold, and it will increase at regular intervals. The interest added by the moneylender will add to the increase of the principal. I know a sandal maker named Ansan who told me that each week for eight years he had deposited two pieces of silver with his moneylender. The moneylender recently gave Ansan the interest earned by his silver contributions, and he was pleased to see how much money he'd earned. His small deposits, at the customary interest rate of one-fourth their value for each four years, was now one thousand and forty pieces of silver.

"I encouraged him further by explaining to him with my knowledge of numbers that in twelve years, if he kept his regular deposits of two pieces of silver each week, the moneylender would owe him four thousand pieces of silver, which would sustain him for the rest of his life.

"When someone deposits such a small amount of money at regular intervals and a reasonable profit is returned, no one can afford not to do so; to guarantee money for one's old age and for their family, no matter how successful their business and investments may be.

"I believe one day some smart people will come up with a way to insure against death, whereby people pay just a small amount of money regularly, creating a hefty savings for the family of each member who passed away. I think this would be a great idea, which I would highly recommend.

"Today, however, this is not possible because it would take more than a lifetime to organize and operate such a thing. This would need to be a very stable and trustworthy program. I think that this can happen sometime further in the future and it will benefit so many people when it does. But because we live in the present and not the future, we need to take advantage of the ways to acquire wealth that I have already discussed. I recommend to everyone that they thoughtfully save enough money for their later years. It would be sad for someone to no longer be able to provide for themselves and their family because they didn't save their money as a young person.

"This, then, is the sixth cure for a lean purse: Save enough money in advance to provide for yourself and your family when you are no longer able to earn money."

The Seventh Cure: Increase your ability to earn

Arkad said on the final day of his teaching, "Today I will tell you one of the most vital remedies for a lean purse. I will not talk about gold, but about you people who sit in front of me today. I will tell you what is in the minds and lives of people who work for or against their success."

"Not long ago, a young man came to me hoping to borrow money. When I asked him why he needed money, he complained that he didn't earn enough to pay his expenses. So I explained to him that he was a bad customer for the moneylender, since he had no surplus earning capacity to repay the loan. 'What you need, young man,' I told him, 'is to earn more money. What do you do to increase your capacity to earn?'

"'All that I can do,' he replied. 'I asked my boss six times in two months for a raise, but he hasn't given me one. I can't ask more often than that.'

"We may smile at his simplicity, yet he possessed one of the vital requirements to acquire wealth. Within him was a strong desire to earn more—this is commendable. Before accomplishing something, one must have a desire to accomplish it. Your desires must be strong and definite. General desires are just weak wishes—wishing to be rich will accomplish nothing. On the other hand, wanting to have five pieces of gold is a more tangible goal that is more likely to be reached. After backing your desire for five pieces of gold with the determination to earn it, you can next find similar ways to earn ten pieces and then twenty pieces and later a thousand pieces of gold. Before you know it, you're rich. In learning to secure your one small tangible desire, you will train yourself to secure a larger one. This is the process by which wealth is accumulated: first in small sums, then in larger sums as one learns and becomes more capable. Desires must be simple and tangible. They defeat their own purpose if there are too many, if they're too confusing, or unattainable.

"As one perfects themselves in their career, their ability to earn increases. When I was a humble scribe carving clay for a few coppers a day, I observed that other workers did more and were paid more. I decided that I wouldn't let anybody inferior to me at work pass me up and I figured out the reason for the success of my superiors. I became more interested in my work, concentrated harder on my tasks, and persisted with more effort. After a while, there were few people who could carve more tablets in a day than I could. My increased skill was eventually rewarded, and I didn't even need to ask my boss for a raise.

"The more wisdom we have, the more we can earn. If you want to learn more and get better at your job, you will be rewarded. If you're an artisan, you may seek to learn the methods and the tools of those most skilled in your field. If you are a lawyer or a doctor, you might consult and exchange knowledge with other lawyers and doctors. If you're a merchant, you may continually look for better goods that can be purchased at lower prices, earning you a greater profit.

"The responsibilities of a clever person will often change and improve because they work to improve their skills. I encourage all of you to keep up with the latest developments in your field so you won't be left behind. Many things can make one's life rich with good experiences. If you respect yourself, you must do the following:

"Pay your debts on time, and do not purchase things you cannot afford;

"Take care of your family so that they respect you;

"Have a will made so that your property and assets will be properly and honorably distributed upon your passing;

"Have compassion on those who are ill or less fortunate and help them whenever you can. Do good deeds to those you care about.

"To conclude, the seventh and final remedy for a lean purse is to grow and improve your talents, to study and become wiser, to become more skillful, and to respect yourself. That way you will have enough confidence to achieve your goals.

"Those were the seven cures for a lean purse, which, out of the experience of a long and successful life, I encourage all of you who want to be rich to follow. There is more money in Babylon than you can imagine, my students. There is abundance for all.

"Now practice what I have taught you and grow your wealth—it is your right. Share what I have taught you so that everyone in Babylon can have a part of the ample wealth of our beloved city."

Meet the Goddess of Good Luck

"If a person is lucky, there is no way to predict the potential of their good fortune. Throw them into the Euphrates River and they will probably swim out with a pearl in their hand."

—Babylonian Proverb.

The desire to be lucky is universal. It was just as strong in the hearts of people four thousand years ago in ancient Babylon as it is in the hearts of people today. We all hope to be favored by the whimsical Goddess of Good Luck.

Is there some way we can meet her and attract, not only her favorable attention, but her generous favors? Is there a way to attract good luck? That is just what the people of ancient Babylon wanted to know. It is exactly what they decided to find out. They were intelligent people and keen thinkers, which is why their city became the richest and most powerful city of their time.

In that distant past, they had no schools or colleges, but rather a very practical center of learning. Among the towered buildings of Babylon was one that was equal in importance with the Palace of the King, the

Hanging Gardens, and the temples of the gods. You will find little to no mention of it in the history books, yet it exerted a powerful influence upon the thought of that time.

This building was the Temple of Learning, where the wisdom of the past was shared by voluntary teachers and where subjects of popular interest were discussed in open forums. Within its walls all people met as equals. The humblest of slaves could dispute with immunity the opinions of a prince of the royal house.

Among the many who frequented the Temple of Learning, was a wise and rich man named Arkad, called the richest man in Babylon. He had his own special hall where almost any evening a large group of people, some old, some young, but mostly middle-aged, gathered to discuss and argue interesting subjects. Suppose we listen in to see whether they knew how to attract good luck.

The sun had just set like a great red ball of fire shining through the haze of desert dust when Arkad strolled to his accustomed platform. Eighty people filled the room awaiting his arrival, reclining on their small rugs spread out on the floor. More were still arriving.

"What will we discuss tonight?" Arkad inquired.

After a brief hesitation, a tall cloth weaver addressed him, arising as was the custom. "There is a topic I would like to discuss tonight, but I am afraid to share it because I'm sure it will sound ridiculous to you, Arkad, and my good friends here."

Upon being urged to offer it, both by Arkad and by calls from the others, he continued: "I've been lucky today—I found a purse full of gold. I hope my luck will continue, and, seeing as everyone wishes to be lucky, I think we should discuss how to attract good luck."

"This is definitely an interesting topic, and I'm glad you brought it up," Arkad commented. "To some, good luck is nothing more than something that would happen by accident, by chance, and would come without any purpose or reason. Others believe that good luck comes from Ashtar, the goddess eager to generously reward those who please her. Now I ask you, what are your thoughts on this? Should we see if there is anything we can do to be visited by good luck?"

"Yes! Yes! Let's talk about it!" responded the growing group of eager listeners.

Arkad continued, "To start our discussion, have any of you had similar experiences to our friend here who found the purse of gold?"

There was a pause and everyone looked around expecting someone to reply, but no one did.

"What, no one?" Arkad said, "then this luck really is rare. Does anyone have a suggestion as to where we should continue our search for luck?"

"I do," spoke a young man in professional clothing, standing up. "When one speaks of luck isn't it natural that their thoughts turn to gambling? Isn't that where we find so many people wishing to find themselves in the goddess of luck's favor, hoping she will bless them with winnings?"

As he resumed his seat a voice called, "Don't stop! Continue your story! Tell us, have you found favor with the goddess while gambling? Did she roll your dice well, filling your purse at the dealer's expense or did she roll badly so the dealer took your hard-earned silver?"

The young man joined the good-natured laughter, then replied, "I'm not ashamed to admit the goddess of good luck seemed not to know I was even there. But what about the rest of you? Have you found her waiting around to roll the dice in your favor? I want to hear your stories and learn from your experiences."

"A wise start," broke in Arkad. "We meet here to consider all sides of each question. To ignore gambling would be to overlook an instinct common to many people — the love of taking a chance with a small amount of silver in the hope of winning a lot of gold."

"That reminds me of the races yesterday," called out another listener. "If the goddess frequently visits the casinos, I'm sure she wouldn't overlook the races where the gilded chariots and horses offer much more excitement. Tell us honestly, Arkad, did she whisper to you to bet on those gray horses from Nineveh yesterday? I was standing right behind you and could hardly believe my ears when I heard you place your bet on the gray horses. You know as well as any of us that no team in Assyria can beat our Clydesdales in a fair race. Did the goddess tell you to bet on the grays because at the last turn the inside black horse would stumble and interfere with our Clydesdales so that the grays would win the race and score an unearned victory?"

Arkad smiled indulgently at the banter. "Why do we think that the good goddess would take that much interest in my bet in a horse race? To me she is a goddess of love and dignity who finds pleasure in aiding those who are in need and to reward those who are deserving. I don't look for her at the casinos or at the horse races where people lose more gold than they win, but in other places where people are performing worthwhile actions more worthy of reward.

"When farming, trading fairly, or in any occupation you may have, there is an opportunity to make a profit on your efforts and transactions. Maybe you will not all be rewarded every time because sometimes your judgment may be faulty and other times the winds might defeat your efforts. Yet, if you persist, you can usually expect to find profit. This is because the chances of profit are always in your favor.

"But, when you gamble, the situation is reversed and the chances of profit are always against you and in favor of the dealer. The game is arranged so that it will always favor the dealer. This is the dealer's business at which he plans to make a liberal profit for himself from the coins bet by the players. Few players realize how certain the dealer's profits are and how unlikely they will win.

"For example, let's consider bets placed on a dice roll. Each time it is rolled we bet on which number it will land. If you bet on six and it lands on a six, the dealer pays you four times your bet. But if it lands on any of the other numbers, you lose your bet. So the figures show that for each roll you have five chances to lose, but because the number you bet on pays four for one, you have four chances to win. In one night the dealer can expect to keep one-fifth of all the coins wagered by the gamblers, thus profiting each night. Can someone expect to win often against odds arranged so that they would lose one-fifth of all their bets?"

"But some people sometimes do win a lot of money," volunteered one of the listeners.

"Yes, they do," Arkad continued. "With this in mind, I ask you to consider whether money won by gambling brings permanent value to the lucky winner. Many of my friends are the most successful men in Babylon, but among them I can't name a single one who started his success by winning a bet.

"All of you here know many more of our city's wealthy citizens. To me it would be interesting to learn how many of the citizens of Babylon can credit gambling as their start to success. Can any of you tell how a wealthy person you know earned their riches?"

After a prolonged silence, someone ventured, "Can our answers include dealers at the casino?"

"If you can't think of anyone else," Arkad responded. "If none of you can think of anyone else, then how about yourselves? Are there any lucky people here who hesitate to share where they get their incomes?"

His challenge was answered by a series of groans from the rear taken up and spread amid much laughter.

"It seems like we are not seeking good luck in the places the goddess frequents," he continued. "So let's consider some other fields. We haven't found it by picking up lost wallets, and we haven't found it at the casinos. As for the races, I admit I have lost far more coins there than I have ever won. Now, suppose we consider our jobs and businesses. If you conclude a profitable transaction, you think of it as a reward for your efforts, not good luck, right? I am inclined to think we may be overlooking the gifts the goddess gives us. Perhaps she really does help us when we don't appreciate her generosity. What are your thoughts?"

Thereupon an elderly merchant arose, smoothing his refined white shirt. "With your permission, Arkad and friends, I would like to offer a suggestion. If, as you have said, we take credit for our own business success, why don't we consider the successes we almost had but escaped us? Successes that would have been profitable. They would have been rare examples of good luck if they had actually happened. But because these successes escaped us and brought no fulfillment, we can't consider them rewards. I'm sure many of you here can relate."

"This is a wise point you bring up," Arkad approved. "Have any of you had good luck in your grasp only to see it escape?"

Many hands were raised, among them that of the merchant. Arkad motioned to him to speak. "Since you brought up this point, let's hear from you first."

"I will gladly share a story," the merchant resumed, "that demonstrates how close we can get to good luck and how blindly we let it escape, leading to loss and regret.

"Many years ago, when I was a young man, newly married and working at my first job, my father came one day and told me I should make a particular investment. The son of one of his good friends noticed an empty plot of land just outside the city. It was high above the canal where no water could reach it. The son of my father's friend planned to purchase this land, build three large water wheels that could be operated by cattle, thus bringing the water up to the fertile soil. Once he accomplished this, he planned to divide the land into small plots and sell it to the residents of the city to use as herb gardens.

"The son of my father's friend didn't have enough gold to go through with his plan, seeing as he was a young man who had just started earning money, and did not come from a wealthy family. He decided to recruit a group of people to enter into business with him. Each member in this group of twelve would loan the son money and agree to pay one-tenth of their earnings into the business venture until the land was ready to sell. Everyone would then share the profits in proportion to their investment.

"'My son,' said my father, 'you are now a young man. I would like you to begin building a valuable estate so that you may become a respected man. I want to see you profit from my mistakes.' I replied, 'That is my greatest desire.'

"'Then, I recommend you do this. Do what I should have done at your age. Keep one-tenth of your earnings to put into investments. With this one-tenth of your earnings and the interest it will earn, before you're my age, you can accumulate a valuable estate for yourself.'

"'Thank you for your wise advice, father. I do really want to be rich, but there are so many things I need to use my money for right now, so I hesitate to take your advice. I am young, there is plenty of time.'

"'That's what I thought at your age, but look at me now; many years have passed and I don't have anywhere near as much as I need to sustain myself in my old age.'

"'We are from different generations, father. I will avoid your mistakes.'

"'You have so many opportunities, my son. This is a chance you can take that will lead to wealth. Please do not delay. Tomorrow you should go to the son of my friend and bargain with him to pay ten percent of your earnings into this investment. Go immediately tomorrow—opportunity waits for no one.'

"In spite of my father's advice, I hesitated. The tradesmen brought nice, beautiful, rich clothes from the East and I bought some for my wife and myself, instead of investing my money. If I agreed to pay one-tenth of my earnings into the business venture, we would have to deprive ourselves of these and other pleasures we desired. I delayed making a decision until it was too late, which I came to regret. The business venture proved to be more profitable than anyone predicted. That was my story of how I let good luck get away."

"In this story we see how good luck waits to come to the one who accepts opportunity," commented a man from the desert. "When it comes to building an estate, there is always a beginning. That beginning may be a few pieces of gold or silver that one diverts from their earnings to their first investment. I own a lot of cattle. When I was a young boy I purchased my first calf with one piece of silver. Since this was the beginning of my wealth, it was very important to me.

"Taking the first step in building an estate is the best luck that could come to anyone. That first step, which changes you from a person who earns from your hard work to a person who earns from the interest their gold earns, is important. Some people take this first step when they're young, gaining financial success quicker than those who take the first step later in life, or those unfortunate people, like the father of this merchant, who never take the step.

"If our friend, the merchant, took this step as a young man when this opportunity came to him, today he would be blessed with riches. If the good luck of our friend, the cloth weaver, causes him to take such a step at this time, it will be just the beginning of much greater good fortune."

"I'd like to speak, also." A stranger from another country rose. "I am from Syria and do not speak your language well. I wish to call this merchant a name, but I don't know your word for it. If I say it in my language, you won't understand. Can anyone tell me the right name to call a person who puts off doing things that are good for them?"

"Procrastinator," called a voice.

"That's it," shouted the Syrian, waving his hands excitedly, "he accepts no opportunity when it comes. He waits. Opportunity will not wait for such a slow fellow. If someone desires to be lucky he will step quickly. Anyone who does not step quickly when opportunity comes, is a big procrastinator like our friend, this merchant."

The merchant rose and bowed good naturedly in response to the laughter. "My admiration to you, stranger within our gates, who does not hesitate to speak the truth."

"Let's hear another tale of opportunity—does anyone else have a story?" asked Arkad.

"I have a story," responded a middle aged man. "I buy animals, mostly camels and horses, sometimes sheep and goats. The tale I am about to tell will show how opportunity came one night when I least expected it. Maybe this is the reason I let it escape. You'll be the judge.

"Returning to the city one evening after a disheartening ten day journey in search of camels, I was angered to find the gates of the city closed and locked. While my slaves set up our tent for the night, I was approached by an elderly farmer who, like ourselves, found himself locked outside.

"'Good sir,' he addressed me, 'from your appearance, it looks like you are a buyer. If this is so, I would like to sell you the most excellent flock of sheep. My wife lies very sick with a fever and I need to return to her quickly. If you buy my sheep, my slaves and I can mount our camels and travel back quickly.'

"It was dark so I could not see his flock, but from the bleating I could tell it was large. Since I had searched unsuccessfully for camels for ten days, I was pleased to bargain with him. In his anxiety, he set a reasonable price, which I accepted, knowing my slaves could bring the flock through the city gates in the morning and sell it at a substantial profit.

"I called my slaves to bring torches and count the flock. I won't burden you, my friends, with a description of how difficult it was counting so many thirsty, restless, confused sheep. It turned out to be an impossible task. So I bluntly told the farmer I would count the sheep at daylight and pay him then.

"'Please, most honorable sir,' he pleaded, 'pay me two-thirds of the price tonight so I can go back home. I will leave my most intelligent and educated slave to help with counting in the morning. He is trustworthy and you can pay the balance to him.'

"But I was stubborn and refused to make payment that night. The next morning, before I woke up, the city gates opened and four buyers rushed out in search of flocks. They were eager and willing to pay high prices because times were hard in the city. The farmer ended up receiving nearly three times the money he asked from me. So that's my rare good luck that I let escape."

"This is certainly an unusual story," commented Arkad. "What can we learn from this?"

"Make a payment immediately when you know you're getting a good bargain," suggested a respected saddle maker. "If the bargain is good, then you need protection against your own weaknesses as much as against any other person. We mortals are changeable. I must say it is easier to change our minds when right than wrong. Wrong, we are stubborn. Right, we are prone to change our minds and let opportunity escape. My first judgment is usually my best. Yet, I have always found it difficult to proceed with a good bargain when made. So as a protection against my own weaknesses, I go with my gut and make a payment immediately. This saves me from later regrets when I let good luck pass me up."

"I'd like to speak again." The Syrian man was standing once more. "These tales are very similar; each time opportunity flies away for the same reason. The goddess of good luck comes to a procrastinator with a good plan, the procrastinator hesitates, saying 'right now is not the best time.' How can people succeed that way?"

"You have wise words, my friend," responded the buyer. "Good luck fled from procrastination in both stories—this is not unusual. We are all prone to procrastination. We desire riches, but when opportunity appears before us, our urge to procrastinate encourages us to come up with various reasons to delay. When following the urge to procrastinate, we become our own worst enemies.

"When I was younger, I didn't know that what I was doing was procrastination. At first I thought it was my own poor judgment that caused me to lose profitable opportunities. Later, I credited it to my stubborn disposition. Eventually, I realized what it was: a habit of needless delaying where prompt and decisive action was required. I hated myself when I realized I was procrastinating. With the bitterness of a wild donkey hitched to a chariot, I broke loose from this enemy to my success."

"I'd like to ask Mr. Merchant a question," the Syrian man said. "You wear handsome clothes, not like those of a poor man. You speak like a successful man. Tell us, do you listen now when procrastination whispers in your ear?"

"Like our friend the buyer, I also had to recognize and conquer procrastination," responded the merchant. "To me, it was an enemy, always watching and waiting to make it more difficult to accomplish anything.

"The story I told is similar to stories I could tell to show how it drove away my opportunities. Procrastination is not difficult to conquer, once understood. No one willingly allows a thief to rob them, nor does anyone willingly allow an enemy to drive away their customers and take their profits. When I recognized these acts that my enemy was committing, I conquered him. Everyone must master their own spirit of procrastination before they can expect to share in the rich treasures of Babylon.

"What do you have to say about this, Arkad? Because you are the richest man in Babylon, many say you're also the luckiest. Do you agree with me that no one can really succeed until they have completely crushed the spirit of procrastination within them?"

"Yes, I agree," Arkad admitted. "During my long life I have watched generation after generation following paths of science, business, and academia that lead to success in life. Opportunities came to all these people. Some grasped theirs and were able to reach their goals, but the majority hesitated, faltered, and fell behind." Arkad turned to the cloth weaver. "You suggested that we discuss good luck. What do you have to say on the matter?"

"I see good luck in a different light. I thought of it as something desirable that might happen to someone without effort on their part. Now I realize you can't just attract good luck to yourself. From our discussion I learned that to find good luck, it is necessary to take advantage of opportunities. From here on out I will make the best of the opportunities that come to me."

"That summarizes our discussion well," Arkad replied. "Good luck often follows opportunity but rarely comes otherwise. Our merchant friend would have found good luck if he accepted the opportunity the goddess of luck presented to him. Our friend, the buyer, likewise would have enjoyed good luck if he completed the purchase of the flock of sheep and sold them, making a handsome profit.

"We pursued this discussion to find a way to attract good luck, and I feel we have found the way. Both stories we heard illustrated how good luck follows opportunity. In that illustration lies a truth; a truth that many similar stories of good luck, won or lost, could not change. The truth is this: Good luck can be found by accepting opportunity. Those eager to grasp opportunities to better themselves attract the interest of the good goddess of luck. She is excited to aid those who please her. People of action please her best. Action will lead you forward to achieve your goals."

PEOPLE OF ACTION ARE FAVORED BY THE
GODDESS OF GOOD LUCK.

The Five Laws of Gold

"If you had to choose a bag full of gold or a tablet carved with words of wisdom, which would you choose?"

By the flickering light of a fire made from desert shrubs, the sun-tanned faces of the listeners gleamed with interest.

"The gold," chorused the twenty-seven listeners.

Old Kalabab smiled knowingly. "Listen to the wild dogs out there in the dark," he resumed, raising his hand. "They howl and wail because they are hungry. If we feed them though, they would fight and strut, giving no thought to tomorrow.

"We humans are the same way. Give us a choice of gold or wisdom and what do we do? Ignore the wisdom and waste the gold. Then tomorrow you will complain because you have no more gold. Gold is reserved for those who know its laws and follow them."

Kalabab pulled his robe tightly around him, for a cool night wind was blowing.

"Because you were loyal to me on our long journey, did a good job taking care of my camels, worked hard across the hot sands of the desert without complaining, and bravely fought the robbers who wanted to steal my merchandise, tonight I will tell you the story of the five laws of gold—you have never heard a story like this before. Listen and pay attention to what I'm about to say. If you understand what I tell you, you will come to have a lot of gold in the future."

He paused impressively. Above, in a canopy of blue, the stars shone brightly in the crystal clear skies of Babylonia. Behind the group loomed their faded tents, tightly staked against possible storms. Beside the tents were neatly stacked bales of merchandise covered with skins. Nearby, the camel herd sprawled in the sand, some chewing their cud contentedly, others snoring in hoarse discord.

"You've told us many good stories, Kalabab," spoke up the chief packer. "We will listen closely to your wisdom to guide us tomorrow when we will no longer work for you."

"I have told you about my adventures in strange and distant lands, but tonight I will tell you about the wisdom of Arkad, the wise rich man."

"We've heard of him," acknowledged the chief packer. "He was the richest man who ever lived in Babylon."

"Yes, he was the richest man, and that was because he was wise in the ways of gold; in a way nobody before him had been. Tonight I will tell you about his great wisdom as it was told to me by Nomasir, his son, many years ago in Nineveh, when I was a child:

My master and I had traveled long into the night to get to Nomasir's palace. I helped my master bring bundles of fine rugs, and Nomasir was going to try each one until he found one he liked. He eventually chose one and told us to sit with him and drink a rare liquor that had a strong odor and felt warm in my stomach. Then, he told us this tale of the great wisdom of Arkad, his father, just as I will tell it to you.

In Babylon it is tradition, as you know, that the sons of wealthy individuals live with their parents in expectation of inheriting the estate. Arkad did not approve of this tradition. Therefore, when Nomasir was old enough to inherit the estate, Arkad said to his son, "My son, I want you to inherit my estate. However, you must first prove that you are capable of handling it wisely. So, I ask you to go out into the world and show your ability both to acquire gold and to make yourself respected among men. To start you off, I will give you two things that I didn't have when I started as a poor young man.

"First, I give you this bag of gold. If you use it wisely, it will be the basis of your future success. Second, I give you this clay tablet carved with the five laws of gold. If you apply them to your daily life, they will bring you knowledge and safety. In ten years, come back to my house and tell me how you did. If you do a good job, I will make you the heir to my estate. Otherwise, I will leave it to the priests to hand over to the gods so that my soul may be saved."

So Nomasir went, taking his bag of gold, the clay tablet carefully wrapped in cloth, his slave, and his horses.

The ten years passed and Nomasir, as he agreed, returned to his father's house, who threw a party for his son with all of his friends and relatives. When the party was over, Nomasir's father and mother mounted their throne-like seats at one side of the great hall, and Nomasir stood in front of them to tell them about his last ten years. It was evening. The room was hazy with smoke from the wicks of the oil lamps that provided a dim light. Slaves in white outfits fanned the humid air rhythmically with long-stemmed palm leaves. The scene had a look of royalty to it. Nomasir's wife and two young sons, as well as some other friends and family members sat on the rugs behind him, listening eagerly.

"My father," he began respectfully, "I bow before your wisdom. Ten years ago, when I was just a young man, you told me to go and become a man among men, instead of remaining a subject to your fortune. You gave me a generous amount of gold, and you shared your wisdom.

"I must admit I handled the gold poorly; it fled out of my inexperienced hands the same way a wild rabbit flees at the first opportunity from the child who captures it."

The father smiled indulgently. "Continue, my son. Your story interests me in all its details."

"I decided to go to Nineveh, as it was a growing city, believing that I might find opportunities there. I joined a caravan and made a lot of friends, two of whom were well-spoken men with a beautiful white horse. As we journeyed, they told me secretly that there was a wealthy man in Nineveh who owned a horse so fast that it had never been beaten.

Its owner believed that no other horse could run faster. Therefore, he would bet any amount money that his horse could outrun any other in Babylonia. Compared to their horse, so my friends said, it was a lumbering donkey that could be beaten with ease. As a great favor, they let me join them in placing their bets. I got carried away with the plan.

"Our horse was badly beaten and I lost a lot of my gold." The father laughed. "Later, I discovered that this was a deceitful plan of these people and they constantly journeyed with caravans seeking victims. You see, the man in Nineveh was their partner and shared with them the bets he won. This trick played on me taught me my first lesson in looking out for myself.

"I quickly learned another lesson, equally bitter. In the caravan was another young man whom I befriended. He was the son of wealthy parents and, like myself, was traveling to Nineveh to find a place to live. Not long after our arrival, he told me that a merchant had died and his shop, full of profitable merchandise and loyal customers, was being sold at a bargain price. He said that we would be equal partners after he returned to Babylon to get his gold. He persuaded me to purchase the shop with my gold, agreeing that his own gold would be used later to continue funding our business.

"He put off going back to Babylon to get his gold, proving in the meantime to be an unwise buyer and a foolish spender. I finally decided to part ways with him, but not before the business had deteriorated to the point where we only had unsalable merchandise and no gold to buy other goods to sell. I sold the shop for a pitiful amount.

"After that came difficult days. I looked unsuccessfully for a job, as I didn't have any experience or training. I sold my horses, my slave, and my extra clothes so that I could have food and a place to sleep, but poverty inched closer to me each day.

"But in those difficult days, I remembered your confidence in me, father. You sent me out to become a man, and I was determined to accomplish this." The mother covered her face and cried softly. "At this point, I remembered the tablet you gave me with the five laws of gold. So

I carefully read your words of wisdom, and realized that if I had sought wisdom first, I wouldn't have lost my gold so quickly. I memorized each law and decided that, when I came into money again, I would be guided by the wisdom of age and not by the inexperience of youth. For you who are seated here tonight, I will read the wisdom of my father:

THE FIVE LAWS OF GOLD

I.   Gold comes freely and exponentially to anyone who saves at least one-tenth of their earnings to create an estate for their future.
II. Gold multiplies when invested properly.
III. Gold stays with the cautious owner who invests it per the advice of experienced people.
IV. Gold slips away from the person who invests it in businesses or purposes with which they are unfamiliar or that are not approved by experienced advisors.
V.   Gold leaves the person who forces it to impossible earnings or who follows the enticing advice of greedy schemers or who trusts it to their own inexperience and idyllic desires in investment.

"These are the five laws of gold according to my father. I believe they are more valuable than gold itself, as you will come to see as I continue my story."

He again faced his father. "I have told you about the poverty and despair my inexperience brought me. However, there is no chain of disasters that won't eventually come to an end. Mine came when I got a job managing a crew of slaves working on the new outer wall of the city. Profiting from my knowledge of the first law of gold, I saved a copper from my first earnings, adding to it with each paycheck until I had a piece of silver. It took a while, since I had to pay for food and everything else. I was frugal because I was determined, before my ten years were up, to earn as much gold as you, my father, had given me.

"One day the slave master, a new friend of mine, said to me, 'You are a clever young man who doesn't spend much of what he earns. Do you have any gold saved?'

"'Yes,' I replied, 'I want nothing more than to earn enough gold to replace the gold that my father gave me, which I then lost.'

"'Good for you! Did you know that the gold you have saved can work for you and earn interest?'

"'I've had bad experiences with investing my gold in the past. That's how I lost all of my money to begin with.'

"'If you trust me, I will teach you how to handle gold profitably,' he replied. 'Within a year the outer wall will be finished and ready for the bronze gates to be built at each entrance. In all of Nineveh there is not enough metal to make these gates and the King has not provided it. Here is my plan: A group of us will combine our gold and send a caravan to the far-away mines of copper and tin, and bring back the metal for the gates. When the King says, 'Make the grand gates,' we alone will be able to supply the metal and he will be forced to pay us a high price. If the King doesn't buy from us, we will still have the metal that can be sold for a reasonable profit.'

"In his offer I recognized an opportunity to abide by the third law and invest my savings under the guidance of wise men. I was not disappointed; our investment was a success, and my small store of gold was greatly increased by the venture.

"Eventually, I was accepted as a member of this same group in other ventures. This group was full of people who were wise in the profitable handling of gold. They carefully discussed each plan presented before going in on it. They would take no chance of losing their principal or tying it up in unprofitable investments from which their gold could not be recovered. The mistakes I made earlier with the horse races and buying the shop would have quickly been passed up by this experienced group— they would have immediately pointed out their weaknesses. By working with this group, I learned to safely invest gold to bring profitable returns. As the years went on, my treasure increased more and more rapidly. I not only made back the gold I contributed, but much more.

"Through my misfortunes and successes, I have tested the legitimacy of the five laws of gold, and have proven them true in every test. People who don't know about the five laws will lose gold quickly and will not earn it easily. But people who follow the five laws find that gold comes quickly and easily to them."

Nomasir stopped talking and motioned to a slave in the back of the room. The slave brought forward three heavy leather bags. Nomasir took one and placed it on the floor in front of his father, addressing him again: "You gave me a bag of Babylon gold. In its place, I give to you a bag of Nineveh gold of equal weight—an equal exchange. You also gave me a clay tablet with the five laws of gold written on it. In its place, I bring two additional bags of gold." As he said this, he took the other two bags and placed them on the floor in front of his father. "I do this to show you, my father, how much I value your wisdom—it was worth more to me than your gold. Yet, who can measure the value of wisdom in bags of gold? Without wisdom, gold is quickly lost by those who have it, but with wisdom, gold can be secured by the poorest people, as these three bags of gold show. It gives me the greatest satisfaction to stand before you, my father, and say that, because of your wisdom, I am now rich and respected." The father placed his hand fondly on Nomasir's head. "You have learned a lot and I am lucky to have a son I can trust my wealth to."

***

Kalabab ceased his tale and looked critically at his listeners.

"What does the story of Nomasir mean to you?" he continued. "Who among you can go to your father and give an account of how wisely you handled your money? What would these respected men think if you said, 'I have traveled, learned, worked, and earned a lot, yet I have little gold. I spent some of it wisely and some of it poorly.'

"Do you still think it is just an inconsistency of fate that some people have much more gold than others? People have a lot of gold when they know and follow the five laws of gold.

"Because I learned these five laws as a young man and followed them, I have become a wealthy merchant. I didn't accumulate wealth by some strange magic. Wealth that comes quickly goes quickly. Wealth that stays to give enjoyment and satisfaction to its owner comes gradually, because it comes from knowledge and persistent purpose. To earn wealth is just a slight burden on a thoughtful person. Bearing the burden consistently from year to year accomplishes the final purpose.

"The five laws of gold offer a rich reward if you follow them. Each of these five laws is rich with meaning and in case you forgot them during my short story, I'll repeat them now. I know them each by heart because as a young man I saw their immense value, and would not be satisfied until I knew them word for word.

> **The First Law of Gold:** Gold comes freely and exponentially to anyone who saves at least one-tenth of their earnings to create an estate for their future.

"Anyone who saves one-tenth of their earnings consistently and invests it wisely will create a valuable estate that will provide an income for themselves in the future and guarantee safety for their family if they die young. This law says that gold comes readily to such a person, and I can prove this true with my own life. The more gold I accumulate, the more readily it comes to me in greater quantities. The gold I save earns more, and its earnings earn more; this is how the first law works."

> **The Second Law of Gold:** Gold multiplies when invested properly.

"Gold is a willing worker. It is eager to multiply when opportunity presents itself. To everyone who has gold saved, opportunity will come for its profitable use. As the years pass, it will multiply itself."

The Third Law of Gold: Gold stays with the cautious owner who invests it per the advice of experienced people.

"Gold clings to a cautious owner, and flees from the careless owner. Those who seek the advice of people who have experience handling gold learn to use their gold wisely and enjoy its consistent increase."

The Fourth Law of Gold: Gold slips away from the person who invests it in businesses or purposes with which they are unfamiliar or that are not approved by experienced advisors.

"Anyone who has gold but is not skilled at handling it will find many uses for it, all of which appear profitable. These are often not profitable and lead to loss. The inexperienced owner of gold who trusts their own judgment and invests it in unfamiliar ventures often finds their judgment imperfect, thus paying for their inexperience. It is wise to seek the advice of people with experience handling gold."

The Fifth Law of Gold: Gold leaves the person who forces it to impossible earnings, or who follows the enticing advice of greedy schemers, or who trusts it to their own inexperience and idyllic desires in investment.

"Exciting opportunities that appear to be thrilling adventures will always come to the new owner of gold. One will think these opportunities will endow their treasure with magical powers that will enable it to make unimaginable earnings. Wise people know the risks that lurk behind every plan to make great wealth suddenly—listen to their warnings. Don't forget the rich people of Nineveh who wouldn't take any chance of losing their principal or tying it up in unprofitable investments.

"That was my story of the five laws of gold. These aren't really secrets but truths that everyone must learn and follow if they hope to not have to worry about whether they will be able to afford their next meal. Tomorrow, we will enter Babylon. Look at the fire that burns eternal above the Temple of Bel! We are already in sight of the golden city. Tomorrow, each of you will have gold, the gold you have each rightfully earned with your loyal services. Ten years from now, what will you be able to say about this gold?

"If any of you, like Nomasir, will use a portion of their gold to start an estate for yourselves and be wisely guided by the wisdom of Arkad, it is safe to assume that ten years from now, like the son of Arkad, you will be rich and respected. Our wise acts follow us through life to please and help us. Similarly, our unwise acts will follow, haunting and tormenting us. Feelings of regret over things we should have done, the opportunities we passed up, will haunt us.

"The treasures of Babylon are so rich that no one can count their value in pieces of gold—these treasures grow richer each year. These treasures are a rich reward for people who are determined to earn their share. There is a magical power in the strength of your own goals and wants. Guide this power with your knowledge of the five laws of gold and you will acquire the treasures of Babylon."

The Gold Lender
of Babylon

Fifty pieces of gold! Never before had Rodan, a spear maker of old Babylon, carried so much gold in his leather purse. He strode happily down the King's highway from the palace of his most generous Majesty. The gold clinked cheerfully as the purse at his belt swayed with each step—the sweetest music he had ever heard.

Fifty pieces of gold! All his! He could hardly believe his good fortune. What power in those clinking coins! They could purchase anything he wanted, a grand house, land, cattle, camels, horses, chariots, whatever he wanted. What should he do with the gold? That evening, as he turned onto a side street toward his sister's house, he could think of nothing he would rather possess than those same glittering, heavy pieces of gold—and they were his to keep!

One evening a few days later, a conflicted Rodan entered the shop of Mathon, a lender of gold and dealer of jewels and rare fabrics. Glancing neither to the right nor the left at the colorful and artfully displayed merchandise, he passed through to the living quarters at the rear. Here he found the respectable Mathon lounging on a rug and eating a meal served by a slave.

"I don't know what to do; can I ask for your advice?" Rodan stood impassively, feet apart, hairy chest exposed by the gaping front of his leather coat.

Mathon's narrow, sallow face smiled a friendly greeting. "What careless actions have you taken that require you to come to the lender of gold? Have you lost money gambling? Are you spending your money in inappropriate ways? I have known you for many years, but you've never come to me for help with your troubles."

"No, no nothing like that. I don't need gold, I just want your wise advice."

"Oh, what a surprise! Nobody comes to the lender of gold for advice. I must have misheard you."

"You heard me right."

"Seriously? Rodan, the spear maker, shows he is more clever than the rest by coming to me not for gold, but for advice. Many people come to me for gold to pay their debts, but nobody asks for advice, even though I am probably the best equipped to give advice to people who are having trouble with gold.

"Have dinner with me, Rodan," he continued, "you'll be my guest this evening." He addressed his slave, "Andol, get a chair for my friend, Rodan, the spear maker, who comes for advice. He will be my honored guest. Bring him a lot of food and get him my largest cup filled with my best wine. Now, tell me what is bothering you," Mathon said to Rodan.

"It is the King's gift."

"The King's gift? The King gave you a gift and it is bothering you? What kind of gift?"

"He gave me fifty pieces of gold because he liked the design I submitted to him for a new point on the spears for the royal guard, and now I don't know what to do. People ask me each hour of the day for me to share my gold with them."

"Your feelings are natural. More people want gold than those who actually have it, and wish that those who have it would share it. But can't you say 'No'? Don't you want to be strong?"

"I can say no to many, but sometimes it is easier to say yes. How can I refuse to share with my sister with whom I am very close?"

"I'm sure your own sister wouldn't want to deprive you of enjoying your reward."

"Well, she's asking because she wants to see her husband Araman become a rich merchant. She feels that he has never had a chance and she wants me to loan him this gold so that he can become a prosperous merchant and then pay me back from his profits."

"My friend," resumed Mathon, "this is definitely a valid concern you bring up. Gold brings responsibility and changes one's position in society. It brings fear that you may lose it in one way or another. It brings a feeling of power and ability to do good. Likewise, it brings opportunities wherein your good intentions may bring troubles.

"Have you ever heard of the farmer of Nineveh who could understand the language of animals? I'll tell you the story so that you know that borrowing and lending is more than the passing of gold from the hands of one to the hands of another.

"This farmer, who could understand what the animals said to each other, lingered in the barnyard each evening just to listen to their words. One evening, he heard the bull complaining to the donkey how difficult his work was: 'I pull the plow from morning till night. No matter how hot it is that day, how tired my legs get, or how heavy the plow feels, I still must work. But you are a creature of leisure. You are covered with a colorful blanket and do nothing more than carry our master where he wants to go. When he doesn't go anywhere, you rest and eat grass all day.'

"The donkey, in spite of being untrustworthy sometimes, was a good animal and sympathized with the bull. 'My good friend,' he replied, 'you do work very hard and I would like to make your work easier, so I will tell you how to have a day off. In the morning when the slave comes to get you to the plow, lie on the ground and cry about how you are sick and cannot work.'

"So the bull took the advice of the donkey and the next morning the slave returned to the farmer and told him the bull was sick and could not pull the plow.

"'Then hitch the donkey to the plow,' said the farmer. 'The field still needs plowing.'

"All day the donkey, who only wanted to help his friend, found himself being forced to do the bull's work. When night came and he was released from the plow, his heart was bitter, his legs were weak, and his neck was sore. The farmer lingered in the barnyard to listen. The bull began speaking first. 'You are a good friend. Because of your wise advice I have enjoyed a day off.'

"'And I,' retorted the donkey, 'am like many other simple-minded animals who start to help a friend and end up doing their work for them. From now on, you will do your own work; I heard the master tell the slave to send you to the butcher if you fell sick again. I wish he would, you lazy fellow.'

"This ended their friendship—they didn't speak to each other any more. What is the moral of the story, Rodan?"

"It was a good story," responded Rodan, "but I don't see a moral."

"I didn't think you would, but there is a simple moral: If you want to help your friend, do so in a way that won't bring their burdens to yourself."

"I hadn't thought of that—that makes sense. I don't want to take on the burdens of my sister's husband. Tell me, you lend to many, do your borrowers repay you?"

Mathon smiled the smile of one whose soul is rich with experience. "Shouldn't the lender be wise and judge carefully whether his gold can perform a useful purpose to the borrower and return to him again? Or whether it will be wasted by someone unable to use it wisely, taking the lender's gold and leaving the borrower with a debt he can't repay? I want to show you the tokens in my chest and let them tell you some of their stories."

He brought a chest, as long as his arm, covered with red pigskin, and decorated with bronze designs, into the room. He put it on the floor and squatted behind it, both hands on the lid.

"From each person to whom I lend, I take a token for my token chest, to remain there until the loan is repaid. When they repay I give their token back, but if they never repay, their token will always remind me of those who were not faithful to my trust.

"The safest loans, my token box tells me, are to those whose possessions are more valuable than the one they desire. They own land, jewels, cattle, or other things that could be sold to repay the loan. Some of the tokens given to me are jewels worth more than the loan. Others are promises that, if the loan is not repaid as agreed, they will bring me a property settlement. On loans like those I am assured that my gold will be returned since the loan is based on property.

"In another group are those who are able to earn—people like you, who labor or serve and are paid. They have an income and if they are honest and have average luck, I know that they too can repay the gold I loan them; such loans are based on human effort.

"Others have neither property nor assured earning capacity. Life is hard and there will always be some who cannot adjust themselves to it. For the loans I give them, even though they are small, my token box may condemn me in the years to come unless they are backed by people who know the borrower is trustworthy."

Mathon opened the lid and Rodan leaned forward eagerly. At the top of the chest a bronze necklace lay on a scarlet cloth. Mathon picked up the necklace and patted it affectionately. "This will always remain in my token chest because the owner died. I treasure his token, and I treasure his memory; he was my good friend. We traded together successfully until he married a beautiful, dazzling woman; he spent his gold lavishly to gratify her desires. He came to me in distress when his gold was gone. I told him I would help him get his finances together again and he swore he would take my advice, but he didn't. While fighting with his wife one day, he was murdered after she stabbed him in the heart."

"And what happened to her?" questioned Rodan.

"This was hers." He picked up the scarlet cloth. "In bitter remorse, she threw herself into the Euphrates River. These two loans will never be repaid. The chest tells you, Rodan, that people going through a passionate time in their life are not safe risks for the gold lender.

"Here! Now, this one is different." He reached for a ring carved of cattle bone. "This belongs to a farmer; I buy rugs from him. The locusts came and the farmer had no food. I helped him and when he was able to grow food again, he repaid me. He came to me again another time and told me about some strange goats in a distant land a traveler told him about. They had long hair so fine and soft it would weave into rugs more beautiful than anything ever seen in Babylon. He wanted a herd of these goats but had no money, so I lent him gold to make the journey and bring back goats. Now he has his herd and next year I will surprise the lords of Babylon with the most expensive rugs they've ever had the pleasure of buying. Soon I need to give his ring back. He insists on repaying me as soon as possible."

"Some borrowers do that?" asked Rodan.

"If they borrow for purposes that bring money back to them, yes. But if they borrow to pay other debts, I warn you to be cautious if you ever want your gold back."

"Tell me about this one," requested Rodan, picking up a heavy gold bracelet inset with jewels in rare designs.

"The women appeal to you, my good friend," bantered Mathon.

"I am still much younger than you," retorted Rodan.

"That's true, but you suspect romance where there is none. The owner of this is fat and wrinkled and talks so much yet has so few things of value to say—she drives me mad. Once, she had a lot of money and was a good customer, but then she encountered some bad times. She has a son whom she wanted to become a merchant. She came to me and borrowed gold so that he could work with a caravan owner who travels with his camels bartering in one city what he buys in another.

"This caravan owner was a rascal, and he left the poor boy in a distant city without money or friends, sneaking away in the early morning while the boy slept. Perhaps when this boy grows into a man, he will repay, but until then I don't earn any money from the loan, just a lot of talk. But I do admit the jewels are worthy of the loan."

"Did this lady even ask you if this loan would be a good idea?"

"Quite the opposite. She pictured her son as a wealthy and powerful man of Babylon. To suggest the contrary would infuriate her. I knew the risk for this inexperienced boy, but since she offered security I could not refuse her.

"This," continued Mathon, waving a bit of pack rope tied into a knot, "belongs to Nebatur, the camel trader. When he wanted to buy a herd larger than his funds he brought me this knot and I lent him the money he needed. He is a wise trader. I have confidence in his good judgment and can lend him money freely. Many other merchants of Babylon have my trust because of their honorable behavior. Their tokens come and go frequently in my token box. Good merchants are an asset to our city and loaning them money brings me profits and helps Babylon remain prosperous."

Mathon picked out a beetle carved in turquoise and tossed it on the floor, disgustedly. "This is a bug from Egypt. The man who owns this does not care whether I ever receive back my gold. When I question him, he replies, 'How can I repay you when I am followed by bad luck? You have plenty more.' What can I do? The token is his father's—a worthy man with little money who pledged his land and cattle to back his son's enterprises. The young man found success at first and then was overzealous to gain great wealth.

"His knowledge was immature and his enterprises collapsed. Young people are ambitious and take shortcuts to wealth and the desirable things for which it stands. To secure wealth quickly, young people often borrow unwisely. Young people, having no experience, cannot realize that hopeless debt is like a deep pit into which one may descend quickly and where one may struggle endlessly. It is a pit of sorrow and regrets where the sun never shines and the nights are unhappy and restless. Yet, I still encourage borrowing gold if it is for a wise purpose. I made my first real success as a merchant with the gold I borrowed. But what should a lender do in my situation? The young man is in despair and accomplishes nothing. He is discouraged and makes no effort to repay, but I hate to deprive the father of his land and cattle."

"You've told me some interesting stories," ventured Rodan, "but, you haven't answered my question. Should I lend fifty pieces of gold to my sister's husband? My sister means a lot to me."

"Your sister is an admirable woman and I have a lot of respect for her. If her husband came to me and asked to borrow fifty pieces of gold I would ask him what he would use it for. If he said that he wanted to become a merchant like myself and deal in jewels and rich furnishings, I would say, 'What do you know about trading? Do you know where you can buy items at the lowest cost? Do you know where you can sell at a fair price?' Could he say 'Yes' to these questions?"

"No, he could not," Rodan admitted. "He has helped me a lot in making spears and has worked in some of the shops."

"Then I'd say to him that his purpose isn't wise. Merchants must learn their trade. His ambition, though worthy, is not practical and I would not lend him any gold. But if he said, 'Yes, I have experience working with merchants. I know how to travel to Smyrna and to buy rugs at a low cost. I also know many of the rich people of Babylon to whom I can sell these at a large profit.' Then I would say, 'Your purpose is wise and your ambition is honorable. I would be glad to lend you the fifty pieces of gold if you can give me security that they will be returned.' But if he says, 'I have no security other than that I am an honored man and will pay you well for the loan.' Then I would reply, 'I treasure each piece of my gold. If the robbers took it from you as you journeyed to Smyrna or took the rugs from you as you returned, then you would have no means of repaying me and my gold would be gone.'

"Gold, you see, Rodan, is the merchandise of the lender of money. It is easy to lend. If it is lent unwisely then it is difficult to get back. The wise lender doesn't want to risk lending their money out if a safe repayment is not guaranteed. It is good, of course, to help those in need, and to help those who are having a difficult time. It is good to help those who are just starting out, so that they may progress and become valuable citizens. But help must be given wisely, or else we will take on the burden of someone else, like what happened with the farmer's donkey.

"I wandered from your question again, Rodan, but hear my answer: Keep your fifty pieces of gold. What you earn from your labors and what is given to you for reward is yours to keep and no one can force you to give away your gold if you don't want to. If you lend it to earn more gold, then lend diversely and with caution. I am unhappy when my gold is unproductive, but even more so when I lose it to a risky cause. How many years have you been a spear maker?"

"Three years."

"How much besides the King's gift do you have saved?"

"Three gold pieces."

"Each year that you have worked you denied yourself luxuries to save one piece of gold from your earnings?"

"Yes."

"Then after working for fifty years wouldn't you have fifty pieces of gold because of this same strategy of self denial?"

"That would be a lifetime of hard work."

"Do you think your sister would want to jeopardize the savings of fifty years of labor over the bronze melting pot so that her husband might experiment with being a merchant?"

"Not when you put it that way."

"Then go to her and say: 'Three years I have worked every day from morning until night, and I have denied myself many luxuries I wanted. For each year of labor and self denial I have earned one piece of gold. I love you and I want your husband to prosper in his business ventures. If he gives me a plan that seems wise and possible to my friend, Mathon, then I will gladly lend him my year's savings so that he has the opportunity to prove that he can succeed.' If he wants to succeed he will be able to prove it. If he fails, he won't owe you anything.

"I am a gold lender because I own more gold than I need. I want my surplus gold to work for others and earn more gold as a result. I don't want to take the risk of losing my gold as I have worked hard and denied myself luxuries to secure it. So I will no longer lend any of it where I am not confident that it is safe and will be returned to me, and I won't lend it where I am not convinced that its earnings will be promptly paid to me.

"I have told you, Rodan, a few of the secrets of my token chest from which you learned the weakness of some and their eagerness to borrow what they cannot repay. From this you can see how often their high hopes of becoming rich are just false hopes, which they don't have the ability or training to fulfill.

"Rodan, you now have gold that you should put to work earning more gold for you. You are about to become a gold lender like me. If you safely preserve your treasure, it will produce liberal earnings for you and be a rich source of pleasure and profit for the rest of your life. But if you let your gold escape from you, it will be a source of constant sorrow and regret. What do you want to do with most of your gold?"

"I want to keep it safe."

"Wisely spoken," replied Mathon approvingly. "Do you think that in the custody of your sister's husband it would be safe from possible loss?"

"He isn't good at guarding gold."

"Then don't be persuaded by foolish sentiments of obligation and trust your treasure to just anyone. If you need to help your family or friends, find other ways that don't risk the loss of your treasure. Don't forget that gold slips away in unexpected ways from those who aren't good at guarding it. Losing your gold by spending it extravagantly and letting others lose your gold for you are equally harmful.

"After safety, what else do you want to do with your gold?"

"To earn more gold."

"Again you speak wisely. Gold should earn and grow larger. Gold wisely lent may even double itself with its earnings before you grow old. If you risk losing your gold, then you risk losing all that it had the potential to earn. So don't be persuaded by the fantastic plans of impractical people who think they know how to make spectacularly large earnings. These plans are the creations of dreamers unskilled in the safe and dependable laws of trade. Be conservative in what you expect it to earn so that you can keep and enjoy your treasure. To hire it out with a promise of unreasonable returns is to invite loss.

"Associate yourself with people and businesses whose success is established so that your treasure earns liberally under their skillful use and is guarded safely by their wisdom and experience. Avoid the misfortunes that follow most of those to whom the gods entrust gold."

When Rodan tried to thank him for his wise advice, he would not listen, saying, "The King's gift will teach you a lot. If you keep your fifty pieces of gold, you must be conservative. Many uses for your gold will tempt you, and many people will try to share advice. You will be offered numerous opportunities to make large profits. The stories from my token box should warn you: Before you let any piece of gold leave your purse, be sure that you have a safe way to pull it back again. If you need any more advice, please come back. I am happy to give it. Before you go, read what I carved under the lid of my token box. It applies equally to the borrower and the lender:

BETTER A LITTLE CAUTION THAN A GREAT REGRET.

The Walls of Babylon

Old Banzar, grim warrior of a bygone day, stood guard at the passageway leading to the top of the ancient walls of Babylon. Up above, valiant defenders were battling to hold the walls. The future existence of this great city with its hundreds of thousands of citizens depended on them.

Over the walls came the roar of the attacking armies: the yelling of many soldiers, the trampling of thousands of horses, the deafening boom of the battering rams pounding the bronzed gates. In the street behind the gate sat the spearmen, waiting to defend the entrance if the gates gave way—he was just one of a few doing this.

The main armies of Babylon were with their King, far away in the east on the great expedition against the Elamites. No attack upon the city had been anticipated during their absence, so the defending forces were small. Unexpectedly, the mighty armies of the Assyrians bore down from the north, and now the walls must hold or Babylon was doomed.

Around Banzar were big crowds of terrified citizens eagerly seeking news of the battle. With hushed awe they viewed the stream of the wounded and dead being carried or led out of the passageway. Here was the crucial point of attack. After three days of circling the city, the enemy had suddenly thrown its great strength against this section and this gate.

The defenders from the top of the wall fought off the siege towers and the wall-scaling ladders of the attackers with arrows, burning oil and, if any reached the top, spears. Thousands of the enemy's archers loosed a deadly barrage of arrows against the defenders.

Old Banzar had the vantage point for news. He was closest to the conflict and first to hear each time the frenzied attackers were repelled. An elderly merchant crowded close to him, his hands trembling. "Tell me! Tell me!" he pleaded. "Tell me they can't get in. My sons are with the good King. There is no one to protect my old wife. They will steal all of my belongings and leave none of my food behind. We are old, too old to defend ourselves—too old to own slaves. We'll starve and die. Tell me they cannot get in."

"Calm down," the guard responded. "The walls of Babylon are strong. Go back to the market square and tell your wife that the walls will protect you and all of your possessions as safely as they protect the rich treasures of the King. Keep close to the walls, or the arrows flying over will hit you!"

A woman with a baby in her arms took the old man's place as he left. "Sergeant, what news do you have? Tell me the truth so I can reassure my poor husband. He has infected wounds and a fever, yet insists on protecting me with his spear and armor. He says that if our enemies break in it will be terrible."

"The tall and strong walls of Babylon will protect you and your baby. Don't you hear the yells of our brave soldiers as they empty the jars of burning oil upon the enemies trying to get in?"

"Yes, I hear that as well as the roar of the battering rams that hammer at our gates."

"Tell your husband the gates are strong and can withstand the rams. Also tell him that the enemies climb the walls but will be impaled by a spear. Now get home safely and quickly."

Banzar stepped aside to clear the passage for heavily armed reinforcements. As they pounded by with their clanking bronze shields, a small girl plucked at his belt.

"Tell me please, soldier, are we safe?" she pleaded. "I hear the awful noises. I see the soldiers all bleeding. I am so scared. What will happen to my family, my mother, little brother, and the baby?"

The grim old campaigner blinked his eyes and thrust forward his chin as he looked at the child.

"Don't be afraid, little one," he reassured her. "The walls of Babylon will protect you, your mother, little brother, and the baby. The good Queen Semiramis built these walls over a hundred years ago for this very purpose—to keep you and your family safe. They have never been broken through. Go back and tell your mother and little brother and the baby that the walls of Babylon will protect them and they don't need to be afraid."

Day after day, old Banzar stood at his post and watched the reinforcements file up the passageway, there to stay and fight until the wounded or dead reinforcements came back down. Around him were unceasingly crowded throngs of frightened citizens eagerly seeking to learn if the walls would hold. To all he gave his answer with the fine dignity of an old soldier, "The walls of Babylon will protect you."

For three weeks and five days the attack raged with unceasing violence. Banzar's visage grew harder and more grim as the passage behind him, wet with the blood of the many wounded, was churned into mud by the endless streams of men marching up and staggering down. Each day the slaughtered attackers piled up in heaps before the wall. Each night they were carried back and buried by their comrades. On the fifth night of the fourth week the chaos finally stopped. The first streaks of daylight, illuminating the plains, revealed great clouds of dust raised by the retreating armies.

A mighty shout went up from the defenders. There was no mistaking its meaning. It was repeated by the waiting troops behind the walls. It was echoed by the citizens upon the streets. It swept over the city with the violence of a storm.

People rushed from their houses. The streets were jammed with a throbbing mob. The fear that was building up for weeks found an outlet in the wild chorus of joy. From the top of the high tower of the Temple of Bel burst forth the flames of victory. Skyward floated the column of blue smoke to carry the message far and wide.

The walls of Babylon had once again repulsed a mighty and vicious foe who was determined to loot her rich treasures and to ravish and enslave her citizens. Babylon endured century after century because it was completely protected. It could not afford to be otherwise. The walls of Babylon were an outstanding example of man's need and desire for protection. This desire is inherent in the human race. It is just as strong today as it ever was, but we have developed broader and better plans to accomplish the same purpose.

In this day, behind the impregnable walls of insurance, savings accounts, and dependable investments, we can guard ourselves against the unexpected tragedies that may enter any door and seat themselves at your table.

WE CANNOT AFFORD TO BE WITHOUT ADEQUATE PROTECTION.

The Camel Trader
of Babylon

The hungrier one is, the clearer one's mind becomes—also the more sensitive one becomes to the odors of food. Tarkad, the son of Azure, certainly thought so. For two whole days he had tasted no food except two small figs stolen from a walled garden. That was all he could grab before he was chased down the street by the angry old woman who owned the trees. Her loud yells were still ringing in his ears as he walked through the marketplace. They helped him to restrain his restless fingers from snatching the tempting fruits from the baskets of the market women.

He had never before realized how much food was brought to the markets of Babylon, and how good it smelled. Leaving the market, he walked across to the inn and paced back and forth in front of the cafeteria. Perhaps here he might see someone he knew; someone from whom he could borrow a copper that would win him a smile from the unfriendly innkeeper and, with it, a generous meal. Without the copper, he knew all too well how unwelcome he would be.

In his daydreaming, he unexpectedly found himself face-to-face with the one man he wished most to avoid: the tall bony figure of Dabasir, the camel trader. Of all his friends and acquaintances from whom he had borrowed small sums, Dabasir made him feel the most uncomfortable because of his failure to keep his promises to repay promptly.

Dabasir's face lit up at the sight of him. "Hey, it's Tarkad, just the one I wanted to see! I've been waiting for my two pieces of copper and a piece of silver that I lent you over a month ago. Good timing, since I need these coins for something today. Do you have my money, kid?"

Tarkad stuttered and his face flushed. His empty stomach deprived him of the nerve he needed to argue with the outspoken Dabasir. "I am sorry, very sorry," he mumbled weakly, "but I don't have the copper or the silver to repay you today."

"Then get it," Dabasir insisted. "Surely, you can find a few coppers and a piece of silver to repay the generosity of an old friend of your father, who helped you when you were in need."

"Bad luck follows me, so I cannot pay you back."

"Bad luck! You're blaming the gods for your own weakness. Bad luck will come to anyone who thinks more of borrowing than of repaying. Come with me while I eat, boy. I am hungry and I would like to tell you a story."

Tarkad flinched from the brutal frankness of Dabasir, but here, at least, was an invitation to enter the coveted doorway of the cafeteria.

Dabasir pushed him to a far corner of the room, where they sat on small rugs. Dabasir addressed Kauskor, the waiter, with his usual freedom, "Fat lizard of the desert, bring me a juicy leg of goat, some bread, and all of the vegetables—I'm hungry and I want a lot of food. And don't forget my friend here. Bring him a bottle of cold water—it's hot out today."

Tarkad's heart sank. Must he sit here and drink water while he watched this man devour an entire goat leg? He said nothing. He thought of nothing he could say. Dabasir, however, was unfamiliar with silence. Smiling and waving his hand good-naturedly to the other customers, all of whom knew him, he continued, "A traveler who just returned from Urfa told me about a certain rich man who had a piece of stone cut so thin that one can see right through it. He put it in the window of his house to keep out the rain. The traveler said it is yellow and that when he looked through it the world looked strange. What do you think about that, Tarkad? Do you think someone could see the world as a different color than it really is?"

"Maybe…" responded the young man, much more interested in the fat goat leg placed before Dabasir than the conversation.

"Well, I know its true since I've seen the world in a different color than what it really is, and the story I am about to tell will show you how I came to see it in its right color again."

"Dabasir is going to tell a story," whispered a neighboring diner to her companion, and dragged her rug close. Other diners brought their food and crowded in a semicircle. They crunched noisily in the ears of Tarkad and gestured around him with their meaty bones. He alone was without food. Dabasir did not offer to share with him, nor even motion for him to take a small corner of the hard bread that was broken off and had fallen from the platter to the floor.

"The story that I am about to tell," began Dabasir, pausing to bite a juicy chunk from the goat leg, "relates to my early life and how I became a camel trader. Did anyone know that I used to be a slave in Syria?"

A murmur of surprise ran through the audience to which Dabasir listened with satisfaction.

"When I was a young man," continued Dabasir after another ferocious bite of goat leg, "my father taught me how to make saddles. I worked with him in his shop before I got married. Just starting out, I didn't earn much—just enough to support my excellent wife. I craved luxurious goods that I could not afford. Soon, I learned that the shop keepers would allow me to pay later since I couldn't pay right away.

"Being young and inexperienced, I didn't know that spending more than I earned is adding fuel to the fire of needless self-indulgence, which will lead to trouble and humiliation. So, I indulged in fine clothes and luxuries for my wife and our home, beyond what we could afford. I paid what I could and for a while all went well. But eventually I discovered that I could not live on my earnings and use them to pay my debts at the same time.

"Creditors began to call and ask me to pay for my extravagant purchases and my life became miserable. I borrowed from my friends, but couldn't repay them either. Things went from bad to worse. My wife left me and I decided to leave Babylon for another city where I might have better chances.

"For two years, I had a restless and unsuccessful life working for caravan traders. After that, I worked with some robbers who scoured the desert for unarmed caravans. I know I was disappointing my family, but I was seeing the world through a colored stone and did not realize the trouble I was in. On our first trip we were successful, gathering a rich haul of gold, silks, and other valuable merchandise. We took these goods to Ginir and wasted the profits we earned.

"The second time we were not so fortunate. Just after we had taken the goods, we were attacked by the soldiers of a native chief, whom the caravans had paid for protection. Our two leaders were killed, and the rest of us were taken to Damascus where we were stripped of our clothing and sold as slaves. I was purchased for two pieces of silver by a Syrian desert chief. My head was shaved, I was given only a loincloth to wear, and I looked exactly like the other slaves. Being a reckless kid, I still thought this was an adventure. That is, until my master took me to his four wives and told them I would be their eunuch. This is when I realized the hopelessness of my situation. These people of the desert were fierce and warlike. I was subject to their will without weapons or a way to escape.

"I stood afraid in front of those four women as they looked at me. I wondered if they would pity me. Sira, the first and oldest wife, looked at me with an indifferent expression. I turned from her, having felt little consolation. The next was an arrogant beauty who gazed at me as if I was a worm. The two younger ones just giggled as though it were all an exciting joke. It seemed like a lifetime that I stood waiting for them to decide my fate. Each woman appeared willing for the others to decide. Finally, Sira spoke up in a cold voice: 'We have plenty of eunuchs, but we could use some new camel handlers—the few we have are worthless. There is not one slave I would trust to lead my camel if I were to travel. Ask this slave if he can lead a camel.'

"My master then asked me, 'What do you know about camels?'

"Striving to conceal my eagerness, I replied that I can make them kneel, I can load them, and I can lead them on long trips without getting tired. If needed, I can even repair their gear and accessories."

"'The slave sounds experienced enough,' observed my master. 'If you want, Sira, take this man as a camel handler.'

"So, I was turned over to Sira and that day I led her camel as it carried her on a long journey to visit her sick mother. I took the occasion to thank her for her intercession. I also told her much of my story—that I was not a slave by birth, but the son of an honorable saddle maker in Babylon.

"Her comments were unsettling and I thought a lot about what she said. 'How can you call yourself a free man when your weakness has brought you to this? If a man has the soul of a slave, he'll become one, even if he was born a so-called free man. If a man has the soul of a free man, he'll be free, becoming respected and honored in his city despite any misfortunes he faces.'

"For over a year I was a slave and lived with the slaves, but I could not become one of them. One day Sira asked me, 'In the evening when the other slaves mingle and enjoy each other's company, why do you sit in your tent alone?'

"I responded, 'I am thinking about what you said to me. I wonder if I have the soul of a slave. I can't join them, so I must sit apart.'

"'I, too, must sit apart,' she confided. 'I came from a wealthy family and my husband married me because of it, yet he does not desire me. What every woman longs for is to be desired. Because of this and because I am unable to have children, I must sit apart. If I were a man I would rather die than be a slave, but the conventions of our tribe make slaves of women.'

"'What do you think of me now?' I asked her suddenly. 'Do I have the soul of a free man or of a slave?'

"'Do you want to repay the debts you owe in Babylon?' she asked.

"'Yes, I want to, but I don't know how I will.'

"'If you passively let the years go by and make no effort to repay, then you have the soul of a slave. Those who cannot respect themselves and repay debts have the soul of a slave.'

"'But what can I do as a slave in Syria?'

"'Stay a slave in Syria, you weakling.'

"'I am not a weakling,' I denied hotly.

"'Then prove it.'

"'How?'

"'Doesn't the great King fight his enemies in every way he can and with every resource he has? Your debts are your enemies—they ran you out of Babylon. You left them alone and they grew too strong for you. If you fought them strongly, you could have conquered them and been honored in your city. But you didn't have the soul to fight them and now you have lost so much confidence that you're a slave in Syria.'

"I thought a lot about her unkind accusations and the defensive things I wish I had said to prove that I was not a slave at heart, but I didn't have the chance. Three days later, Sira's maid brought me to her mistress.

"'My mother is very sick again,' she said. 'Saddle the two best camels in my husband's herd and tie on water skins and saddlebags for a long journey. The maid will give you some food in the kitchen.'

"I packed the camels wondering why the maid gave us so much food even though we only had less than a day's travel. I led Sira's camel and the maid rode the other camel behind her. When we reached her mother's house the sun was just setting. Sira dismissed the maid and said to me: 'Dabasir, do you have the soul of a free man or of a slave?'

"'The soul of a free man,' I insisted.

"'Now is your chance to prove it. Your master and his chiefs are drunk and unaware back in their camp. Take these camels and make your escape. Here in this bag are some of your master's clothes, so you won't be recognized as a slave. I will say you stole the camels and ran away while I visited my sick mother.'

"'You have the soul of a queen,' I told her. 'I wish I could lead you to happiness.'

"'Happiness does not await the runaway wife who seeks it in far-away lands among strangers,' she said. 'Go your own way and may the gods of the desert protect you in the barren landscape.'

"I didn't need any convincing, so I thanked her warmly and quickly left. I didn't know much about this strange country and had only a dim idea of which way Babylon was, but I started bravely across the desert, towards the hills. I rode one camel and led the other. I traveled all night and all the next day, motivated by my knowledge of the terrible punishment handed out to slaves who stole their master's property and tried to escape.

"Late that afternoon, I reached a rough landscape, which was arguably less habitable than the desert. The sharp rocks bruised the feet of my faithful camels and they soon slowed down. I didn't see any people or wildlife, and understood why I found myself alone in such an inhospitable place. From then on, it was the sort of trip few people live to tell of. I ran out of food and water after several days, and the heat of the sun was merciless. At the end of the ninth day, I got off my camel with the feeling that I was too weak to ever get back on and that I would surely die, lost in this desolate wilderness.

"I stretched out on the ground and slept, not waking until the sun had just began to rise. I sat up and looked around. There was a coolness in the morning air and my weary camels lay close by. A vast landscape of broken wilderness covered with rock, sand, and thorny things surrounded me, with no sign of water for myself or my camels. Was I going to die here in this barren tract of land? My mind was more clear than it had ever before been, and my body now felt insignificant. My parched and bleeding lips, my dry and swollen tongue, my empty stomach; the supreme agonies of the day before had disappeared.

"I looked across the uninviting landscape and asked myself once again, 'Do I have the soul of a slave or the soul of a free man?' Then, with clarity I realized that if I had the soul of a slave, I should give up, lie down in the desert, and die. It would be a fitting end for a runaway slave. But if I had the soul of a free man, what then? I would force my way back to Babylon, repay the people who had trusted me, bring happiness to my wife who truly loved me, and bring peace and contentment to my parents.

"'Your debts are your enemies who have run you out of Babylon,' Sira had said. She was right. Why had I refused to stand my ground? Why did I let my actions drive my wife away?

"Then a strange thing happened—the whole world appeared different to me, as though I had been looking at it all this time through a colored stone, which had suddenly been removed. At last, I saw the true values in life. Die in the desert? Not me! With clarity and a new vision, I saw what I needed to do.

"First, I would go back to Babylon and face everyone I owed money to. I would tell them that after years of wandering and misfortune, I had come back to pay my debts as quickly as possible. Next, I would make a home for my wife to come back to and become someone my parents would be proud of. My debts were my enemies, but the people I owed money to were my friends, since they trusted and believed in me.

"I staggered weakly to my feet. It doesn't matter if I'm hungry or thirsty; these were just obstacles on the road to Babylon. The soul of a free man going back to conquer his enemies and reward his friends surged within me, and I was happy.

"The glazed eyes of my camels brightened at the new determination in my husky voice. With great effort, and after many attempts, they got on their feet. With pitiful perseverance, they pushed on toward the north where something within me said we would find Babylon. We eventually found water when we passed into a more fertile country with grass and fruit. We found the trail to Babylon because the soul of a free man looks at life as a series of problems to be solved and solves them, while the soul of a slave whines, 'What can I do? I am just a slave!'

"How about you, Tarkad? Does your empty stomach fill your head with clarity? Are you ready to take the road that leads you back to self-respect? Can you see the world in its true color? Do you want to pay your debts, however many they may be, and once again be a man who is respected in Babylon?"

Tarkad had tears in his eyes as he rose eagerly to his knees. "You have shown me a vision; I already feel the soul of a free man surge within me."

"But what happened when you got home?" questioned one of the intent listeners.

"Where determination is, the way can be found" Dabasir replied. "I now had the determination, so I set out to find a way. First, I visited everyone I owed money to and begged their indulgence until I could earn the money that I needed to repay. Most of them met me gladly, several condemned me, and others offered to help me. Mathon, the gold lender, gave me the help I needed. Learning that I had been a camel trader in Syria, he sent me to old Nebatur, the camel trader, who had just been told by our good King to purchase many herds of strong camels for the great expedition. With him, my knowledge of camels could be put to good use. Gradually, I was able to repay every copper and every piece of silver. Then, at last, I could hold up my head and feel that I was an honorable man."

Again Dabasir turned to his food. "Kauskor, you snail," he called loudly to the kitchen, "the food is cold. Bring me more meat fresh from the roasting. Also, bring a very large portion for Tarkad, the son of my old friend, who is hungry and will eat with me."

So ended the tale of Dabasir the camel trader of old Babylon. He found his own soul when he realized a great truth, a truth that had been known and used by wise people long before his time. It has led people of all ages out of difficulties and into success and it will continue to do so for those who have the wisdom to understand its magic power. It is for anyone who reads these lines.

WHERE THERE IS DETERMINATION, THE WAY CAN BE FOUND.

The Clay Tablets
From Babylon

St. Swithin's College

Nottingham University

Newark-on-Trent

Nottingham

Professor Franklin Caldwell, Care of British Scientific Expedition, Hillah, Mesopotamia

October 21, 1934

My dear Professor:

The five clay tablets from your recent excavation in the ruins of Babylon arrived on the same boat with your letter. I have been fascinated to no end, and have spent many pleasant hours translating their inscriptions. I should have answered your letter more quickly, but waited until I could complete the translations (which are attached).

The tablets arrived without damage, thanks to your careful use of preservatives and careful packing.

You will be as astonished as we in the laboratory were at the story they tell. One expects the dim and distant past to speak of romance and adventure, "Arabian Nights" sort of things, you know? When it instead discloses the financial problems of a person named Dabasir, one realizes that conditions upon this old world have not changed as much in five thousand years as one might expect.

It's odd, you know, but these old inscriptions "discombobulate" me, as the students say. Being a college professor, I am supposed to be a thinking human being possessing a working knowledge of most subjects. Yet, here comes this old chap out of the dust-covered ruins of Babylon to offer a way I had never heard of to pay off my debts, and at the same time acquire gold to jingle in my wallet.

It's a pleasant thought, I say, and should be interesting to prove whether it will work as well nowadays as it did in old Babylon. My wife and I are planning to try out his plan upon our own affairs, which could be much improved. Wishing you the best of luck in your worthy undertaking and eagerly waiting for another opportunity to assist.

Yours sincerely,

Alfred H. Shrewsbury

Department of Archaeology

Tablet No. I:

With the full moon I, Dabasir, who just returned from slavery in Syria, with the determination to pay my many debts and become a man of means worthy of respect in my native city of Babylon, engrave upon this clay a permanent record of my affairs to guide and assist me in carrying through to my goals.

Under the wise advice of my good friend Mathon, the gold lender, I am determined to follow an exact plan that he says will lead any honorable person out of debt and into means and self-respect. This plan has three purposes:

First, the plan will provide for my future prosperity. Therefore, one-tenth of all I earn will be set aside as my own to keep. Mathon spoke wisely when he said:

"The people who keep both gold and silver in their purse that don't need to be spent are good to their family and loyal to their King. The people who have just a few coppers in their purse are indifferent to their family and indifferent to their King. But the people who have nothing in their purse are unkind to their family and are disloyal to their King, for their own hearts are bitter. Therefore, the person who wishes to achieve must have coins that they can keep to jingle in their purse, so they have love for their family and loyalty to their King."

Second, the plan will allow me to support and clothe my good wife who returned to me with renewed loyalty once I escaped slavery. Mathon said that to take good care of a faithful spouse puts self-respect into one's heart and adds strength and determination to one's purposes.

Therefore, seven-tenths of all I earn will be used to provide a home, clothes to wear, and food to eat, with a bit extra to spend, so that our lives are still filled with pleasure and enjoyment. But, it is very important that I do not spend more than seven-tenths of what I earn, even for these worthy purposes. This is where the success of the plan lies. I must live on this portion and never use more or buy what I cannot afford.

Tablet No. II:

Third, the plan provides that my debts should be paid out of my earnings. Therefore, each full moon, two-tenths of all I have earned will be divided fairly among those who have trusted me and to whom I am indebted. With this plan, my debts will soon all be paid off.

I engrave here the names of everyone to whom I am indebted and the honest amount of my debt.

Fahru, the cloth weaver, 2 silver, 6 copper

Sinjar, the couch maker, 1 silver

Ahmar, my friend, 3 silver, 1 copper

Zankar, my friend, 4 silver, 7 copper

Askamir, my friend, 1 silver, 3 copper

Harinsir, the jeweler, 6 silver, 2 copper

Diarbeker, my father's friend, 4 silver, 1 copper

Alkahad, the house owner, 14 silver

Mathon, the gold lender, 9 silver

Birejik, the farmer, 1 silver, 7 copper

(From here on, disintegrated. Cannot be deciphered.)

Tablet No. III:

To these creditors, I owe in total one hundred and nineteen pieces of silver and one hundred and forty-one pieces of copper. Because I owed these sums and saw no way to repay, my wife left me and I left my native city to seek easy wealth elsewhere, only to find disaster and to see myself sold into the degradation of slavery. Now that Mathon showed me how I can repay my debts in small sums of my earnings, I realize the great extent of my mistake in running away from the results of my extravagant spending. Therefore, I have visited my creditors and explained to them that I have no resources with which to pay except my ability to earn,

and that I intend to apply two-tenths of my earnings to my indebtedness evenly and honestly. I can pay this much, but no more. So if they are patient, in time my obligations will be paid in full.

Ahmar, whom I thought was my best friend, attacked me bitterly and I left in humiliation.

Birejik, the farmer, pleaded that I pay him first as he really needed the money.

Alkahad, the house owner, was disagreeable and insisted that he would make trouble for me if I didn't pay him back quickly.

All the rest willingly accepted my proposal. Therefore, I am more determined than ever to carry through, being convinced that it is easier to pay one's debts than it is to avoid them. Though I can't meet the needs and demands of a few of my creditors, I will deal with them all impartially.

Tablet No. IV:

The moon is full again tonight. I have worked hard with a free mind. My good wife has supported my intentions to pay my creditors. Over this past month, because of our wise determination, I have earned nineteen pieces of silver buying camels of sound wind and good legs, for Nebatur. I divided this sum according to my plan: I set aside one-tenth to keep as my own, seven-tenths to pay for my family's living expenses, and two-tenths to pay back my creditors.

I did not see Ahmar but left the money I owed with his wife. Birejik was so pleased he kissed my hand. Old Alkahad alone was grouchy and said I must pay faster, to which I replied that if I were permitted to be well fed and have no worries, that alone would enable me to pay faster. All the others thanked me and spoke well of my efforts. At the end of one month, my debt was reduced by almost four pieces of silver and I have almost two pieces of silver in my savings. My heart is lighter than it has been for a long time.

Again the moon shines full. I have worked hard but with little success. I have been able to buy only a few camels, and have earned eleven pieces of silver. Nevertheless, my good wife and I have stood by the plan even though we have bought no new clothes and eaten little but herbs.

Again, I saved one-tenth of the eleven pieces, while we lived upon seven-tenths. I was surprised when Ahmar and Birejik commended my payment, despite it being small. Alkahad flew into a rage, but when I said I'd be happy to take the payment back if he was unsatisfied, he calmed down and accepted it. The others, as before, were content.

Again the moon shines full and I am greatly rejoiced. I intercepted a fine herd of camels and bought many strong and healthy ones, and earned forty-two pieces of silver. This month my wife and I bought much needed sandals and clothes and dined well on meat and poultry. I paid more than eight pieces of silver to my creditors, and even Alkahad did not protest. This plan is working great, as it is leading me out of debt and is giving me wealth that is mine to keep.

It has been three months since I last carved upon this clay. Each month I saved one-tenth of my earnings, each month my good wife and I lived on seven-tenths, even though at times it was difficult, and each time I paid my creditors two-tenths.

In my purse I now have twenty one pieces of silver that are mine. It makes me feel confident and proud to walk among my friends. My wife keeps our home clean and comfortable and has beautiful clothes to wear—she and I are very happy to live together.

This plan is invaluable—it has made an honorable man of a former slave.

Tablet No. V:

Again the moon shines full and I remember that it has been a year since I first carved on this clay. I felt it was important to carve on the clay today because I have paid the last of my debts. Today, my good wife and I are celebrating with a feast because we met our goal with determination and hard work.

Many things occurred on my final visit to my creditors, which I will never forget. Ahmar begged my forgiveness for his unkind words and said that, out of everyone, I was the one he most desired for a friend. Old Alkahad was not so bad after all, saying, "You were once a piece of soft clay, to be pressed and molded by any hand that touched you, but now you are a piece of bronze capable of holding an edge. If you need silver or gold at any time, come to me."

He is not the only one who holds me in high regard—many others speak my praises. My good wife looks at me with a light in her eyes that gives me so much confidence.

I can only attribute my success to following through on this plan. It enabled me to pay all my debts and still hear the jingle of both gold and silver in my purse. I recommend it to all who wish to get ahead. If it can enable a former slave to pay his debts and have gold in his purse, it can help anyone find financial independence. Though I have met my goal, I am not finished with the plan; I am convinced that if I follow it further it will make me rich.

St. Swithin's College

Nottingham University

Newark-on-Trent

Nottingham

Professor Franklin Caldwell, Care of British Scientific Expedition, Hillah, Mesopotamia

November 7, 1936

My dear professor:

If, in your further digging into those ruins of Babylon, you encounter the ghost of a former resident, an old camel trader named Dabasir, do me a favor. Tell him that his scribbling upon those clay tablets so long ago, has earned for him the lifelong gratitude of a couple of college folks back here in England.

You will probably remember from my writing a year ago that my wife and I intended to try his plan for getting out of debt while still having gold to jingle. You may have guessed, even though we tried to keep it from our friends, our dire straits.

We were frightfully humiliated for years by many old debts and were worried sick for fear that some of the trades-people would start a scandal that would force me out of the college. We paid and paid every shilling we could squeeze out of income, but it was hardly enough to hold things even. Besides, we were forced to do all our buying where we could get further credit, regardless of the higher costs.

It developed into one of those vicious circles that grew worse instead of better. Our struggles were getting hopeless. We could not move to less costly rooms because we owed the landlord. There did not appear to be anything we could do to improve our situation.

Then, here comes your acquaintance, the old camel trader from Babylon, with a plan to do just what we wished to accomplish. He convinced us to follow his system. We made a list of all our debts and I took it around and showed it to everyone we owed.

I explained how it was simply impossible for me to ever pay them with the way things were going. They could readily see this for themselves from the figures. Then, I explained that the only way I saw to pay them back in full was to set aside twenty percent of my income each month to be divided equally, which would pay them in full in a little over two years. That, in the meantime, we would go on a cash basis and give them the further benefit of our cash purchases.

They were really quite decent. Our grocer, a wise old man, put it in a way that helped to bring around the rest. "It is best to pay for all you buy and then pay some of what you owe, since you haven't paid down the account in three years." Finally, I secured all their names to an agreement binding them not to bother us as long as the twenty percent of income was paid regularly.

Then we began scheming on how to live upon seventy percent. We were determined to keep that extra ten percent to jingle. The thought of silver and possibly gold was most alluring. It was like having an adventure to make the change. We enjoyed figuring this way and that, to live comfortably on that remaining seventy percent. We started with rent and managed to secure a fair reduction. Next, we put our favorite brands of tea and such under suspicion and were agreeably surprised how often we could purchase superior qualities at less cost.

It is too long a story for a letter, but anyhow, it did not prove difficult. We managed well. What a relief it proved to have our affairs in such good shape that we were no longer persecuted by past-due accounts.

I must not neglect, however, to tell you about that extra ten percent we were supposed to jingle. Well, we did jingle it for some time. Now don't laugh too soon. You see, that is the sporty part. It is really fun to start accumulating money that you do not want to spend. There is more pleasure in running up a hefty surplus than there could be in spending it.

After we had jingled to our hearts' content, we found a more profitable use for it. We took up an investment upon which we could pay that ten percent each month. This is proving to be the most satisfying part of our regeneration. It is the first thing we pay out of my check.

There is a most gratifying sense of security to know our investment is growing steadily. By the time my teaching days are over it should be a snug sum, large enough so the income will take care of us from then on.

All this out of my same old check. Difficult to believe, yet absolutely true. All our debts are being gradually paid, our investment is increasing, and we get along financially even better than before. Who would believe there could be such a difference in results between following a financial plan and just drifting along.

At the end of the next year, when all our old bills will be paid off, we will have more to pay toward our investment and some extra for travel.

We are determined to never permit our living expenses to exceed seventy percent of our income again. Now you can understand why we would like to extend our personal thanks to that old man whose plan saved us from our "Hell on Earth." He knew. He had been through it all. He wanted others to benefit from his own bitter experiences. That is why he spent tedious hours carving his message in clay. He had a real message for fellow sufferers, a message so important that after five thousand years it has risen out of the ruins of Babylon, just as true and just as vital as the day it was buried.

Yours sincerely,

Alfred H. Shrewsbury

Department of Archeology

The Luckiest Man
In Babylon

Sharru Nada, the merchant prince of Babylon, rode proudly at the head of his caravan. He liked fine cloth and wore rich and luxurious clothes. He liked fine animals and sat easily upon his spirited Arabian stallion. Looking at him, one would never guess how old he was, nor how inwardly troubled.

The journey from Damascus is long and the hardships of the desert are many, but this didn't bother him. The desert tribes are fierce and eager to loot rich caravans. This didn't bother him either, since his many guards were reliable protection.

He was disturbed by the young man at his side, who was travelling with him from Damascus. He felt he owed a debt of gratitude that could never be repaid to Arad Gula, his partner of yesteryear and grandfather to the young man, Hadan Gula. He would like to do something for Hadan, but the more he considered this, the more difficult it seemed because of the young man himself.

Eyeing the young man's rings and earrings, he thought to himself, "He thinks jewels are for men, yet has his grandfather's strong face; his grandfather didn't wear gaudy clothes. Yet, I invited him to come, hoping I could help him get a start for himself and get away from the mess his father has made of their inheritance."

Hadan Gula interrupted his thoughts, "Why do you work so hard, always riding with your caravan on its long journeys? Do you ever take time to enjoy life?"

Sharru Nada smiled. "Enjoy life?" he repeated. "What would you do to 'enjoy life' if you were me?"

"If I had your wealth, I would live like a prince. I'd never ride across the hot desert; I would spend money as fast as it came to my purse; I would wear nice clothes and rare jewels. That's the life I'd live—a life worth living." Both men laughed, but for different reasons.

"Your grandfather didn't wear jewels," Sharru Nada said without thinking, but continued jokingly, "Would you leave any time for work?"

"Work is for slaves," Hadan Gula responded.

Sharru Nada bit his lip but made no reply, riding in silence until the trail led them to the slope. Here, he reined his mount, and pointed to the green valley far away, "There's the valley. Look far down, and you can barely see the walls of Babylon. The tower is the Temple of Bel. If your eyes are sharp, you may even see the smoke from the eternal fire on its crest."

"So, that is Babylon? I have always wanted to see the wealthiest city in the world," Hadan Gula commented. "Babylon, where my grandfather started his fortune. If he were still alive, we would not be in such hardship."

"Why would you want his spirit to linger on earth longer than it should? You and your father can carry on his good work."

"Neither of us have his talent. Father and I don't know his secret for getting so much gold."

Sharru Nada did not reply but gave rein to his mount and rode thoughtfully down the trail to the valley. Behind them, the caravan followed in a cloud of reddish dust. Some time later, they reached the Kings' highway and turned south through the irrigated farms. Three old men plowing a field caught Sharru Nada's attention. They seemed strangely familiar.

How ridiculous! One does not pass a field after forty years and find the same men plowing there. Yet, something within him said they were the same. One, with an uncertain grip, held the plow. The others laboriously worked beside the bulls, ineffectually beating them with their barrel staves to keep them pulling.

Forty years ago he had envied these men! He would have gladly changed places! But what a difference now. With pride, he looked back at his trailing caravan of well-chosen camels and donkeys that was loaded high with valuable goods from Damascus. All of this was but one of his many possessions.

He pointed to the men, saying, "Still plowing the same field where they were forty years ago."

"They sure looks like they've been at it for forty years, but what makes you think they're the same men?"

"I saw them there," Sharru Nada replied. Memories were racing rapidly through his mind. Why could he not bury the past and live in the present? Then he saw, as clear as a picture, the smiling face of Arad Gula. The barrier between himself and the cynical boy beside him dissolved. But how could he help such a superior youth with his spendthrift ideas and bejeweled hands?

He could offer plenty of work to willing workers, but none for people who considered themselves too good for work. Yet, he owed it to Arad Gula to do something, not a half-hearted attempt. He and Arad Gula had never done things that way. They were not that sort of men.

A plan came to him in a flash. He had some objections. He must consider his own family and his own standing. It would be cruel; it would hurt. Being a man of quick decisions, he waived his objections off and decided to act.

"Would you be interested in hearing how your grandfather and I went into a business that became so profitable together?" he questioned.

"Why not just tell me how you became rich? That's all I need to know," the young man parried.

Sharru Nada ignored the reply and continued, "We start with those men plowing. I was no older than you. As I marched in a line with others, good old Megiddo, the farmer, scoffed at the sloppy way in which they plowed. Megiddo was chained next to me. 'Look at the lazy people,' he said, 'the plow holder makes no effort to plow deep, and the beaters are barely keeping the bulls in the row. How can they expect to grow a good crop with poor plowing?'"

"Did you say Megiddo was chained to you?" Hadan Gula asked in surprise.

"Yes, with bronze collars around our necks, and a length of heavy chain between us. Next to him was Zabado, the sheep thief—I knew him in Harroun. At the end was a man we called the Pirate, because he never told us his name. We guessed he was a sailor since he had entwined snakes tattooed on his chest, the way a sailor would. The line of slaves was arranged so we could walk in fours."

"You were chained as a slave?" Hadan Gula asked incredulously.

"Didn't your grandfather tell you I was once a slave?"

"He talked about you a lot, but never told me this."

"He was a man I trusted with my innermost secrets. You, too, are a man I can trust, right?" Sharru Nada looked him squarely in the eye.

"My lips are sealed. Tell me, how did you become a slave?"

Sharru Nada shrugged his shoulders, "Anyone can become a slave. It was the casino and beer that brought me disaster. I was the victim of my brother's mistakes—he killed his friend in a fight. I was bonded to the widow by my father, who was desperate to keep my brother from being prosecuted. When my father could not get enough money to free me, he sold me to the slave dealer."

"That's not fair!" Hadan Gula protested. "But, how did you regain freedom?"

"We'll get to that, but not yet. As we passed, the men jeered at us. One removed his ragged hat and bowed low, calling out, 'Welcome to

Babylon, guests of the King. He waits for you on the city walls where the banquet is spread, mud bricks and onion soup.' With that they laughed cruelly.

"The Pirate flew into a rage and cursed them loudly. 'What do those men mean by the King waiting for us on the walls?' I asked him.

"'You'll march to the city walls to carry bricks until your back breaks. Maybe they'll beat you to death before it breaks. They won't beat me. I'll kill 'em,' the Pirate said.

"Then Megiddo spoke up, 'It doesn't make sense to me, masters beating willing, hard-working slaves to death. Masters like good slaves and treat them well."

"'Who wants to work hard?' commented Zabado. 'Those ploughmen are wise people. They're not breaking their backs—they're just making us think they are.'

"'You can't get ahead by avoiding responsibilities,' Megiddo protested. 'If you plow a hectare, that's a good day's work and any master knows it. But when you plow only a half, you're avoiding your responsibilities. I don't avoid. I like to work and I like to do good work—work is the best friend I've ever known. It has brought me all the good things I've had, my farm and cows and crops, everything.'

"'Yeah, and where are those things now?' scoffed Zabado. 'I figure it pays better to be smart and get by without working. You watch me. If we're sold to the walls, I'll be carrying the water bag or some easy job when you, who likes to work, will be breaking your back carrying bricks.' He laughed his silly laugh.

"I was terrified that night and I couldn't sleep. I got close to the guard rope, and while the others slept, I got the attention of Godoso, who was doing the first guard watch. He was an outlaw, the sort of rogue who, if he robbed you, would think he must also cut your throat.

"'Godoso,' I whispered, 'when we get to Babylon, will we be sold to the walls?'

"'Why do you want to know?' he questioned cautiously.

"'Don't you understand?' I pleaded. 'I am young. I want to live. I don't want to be worked or beaten to death on the walls. Is there any chance for me to get a good master?'

"He whispered back, 'I'll tell you something, since you're a good fellow and you don't give me any trouble. We'll go to the slave market first. When buyers come, tell them you're a good worker, and that you like to work hard for a good master. Make them want to buy. If you don't make them buy, the next day you'll be carrying bricks. The mighty hard work.'

"After he walked away, I lay in the warm sand, looking up at the stars and thinking about work. What Megiddo had said about work being his best friend made me wonder if it would be my best friend. Certainly it would be if it helped me out of this.

"When Megiddo awoke, I whispered my good news to him. It was our one ray of hope as we marched towards Babylon. Late in the afternoon, we approached the walls and could see the lines of people climbing up and down the steep diagonal paths like ants. As we got closer, we were amazed at the thousands of people working; some were digging, others mixed the dirt into mud bricks, most were carrying the bricks in large baskets up the steep trails to the masons.[1]

"Overseers cursed the slow workers and cracked whips over the backs of those who failed to keep in line. Poor, worn-out people were seen to stagger and fall beneath their heavy baskets, unable to get up. If the lash failed to bring them to their feet, they were pushed to the side of the paths and left writhing in agony. Soon, they would be dragged down to join other terrified people lying beside the roadway to await their un-sanctified graves. As I took in the horrible sight, I shuddered. So this was what was waiting for me if I failed at the slave market.

"This force of workers also included many citizens of Babylon and its provinces who had been sold into slavery because of crimes or financial

[1] The famous works of ancient Babylon, its walls, temples, hanging gardens, and great canals, were built by slave labor, mainly prisoners of war, which was the justification for the inhuman treatment they received.

troubles. It was common for people to put themselves, their spouses, or their children up as a promise to guarantee repayment of loans, legal judgments, or other obligations.

"Godoso had been right. We were taken through the gates of the city to the slave prison the next morning and marched to the pens in the market. Here, the rest of the slaves huddled in fear and only the whips of our guard could keep them moving, so the buyers could examine them. Megiddo and I eagerly talked to anyone who would let us. The slave dealer brought soldiers from the King's Guard who shackled the Pirate and brutally beat him when he protested. As they led him away, I felt sorry for him.

"Megiddo thought that we would be separated soon. When no buyers were nearby, he talked to me earnestly to try to convince me how valuable work would be to me in the future, 'Some people hate it and make it their enemy. It is better to treat it like a friend, make yourself like it. Don't mind because it is hard—if you want to build a good house, then who cares if the beams are heavy, and you have to carry materials a far distance. Promise me, boy, if you get a master, work for him as hard as you can. If he does not appreciate all that you do, pay no mind. Remember to work hard, because good comes to hard workers—it will make you a better person.' He stopped as a burly farmer came to the enclosure and looked at us critically. Megiddo asked about his farm and crops, soon convincing him that he would be a valuable man. After violent bargaining with the slave dealer, the farmer drew a fat purse from beneath his robe, and soon Megiddo had followed his new master out of sight.

"A few others were sold that morning. At noon, Godoso confided to me that the dealer was disgusted and would not stay another night and would take all who remained at the end of the day to the King's buyer. I was becoming desperate, when a good-natured man walked up to the wall and asked if there was a baker among us.

"I approached him saying, 'Why should a fine baker like yourself look for an inferior baker? Wouldn't it be easier to teach a willing person like myself your skills? Look at me, I am young, strong, and like to work. Give me a chance, and I will do my best to earn gold and silver for you."

"He was impressed by my willingness and began bargaining with the dealer, who had never even noticed me but now spoke eloquently about my abilities, good health, and good disposition. I felt like a fattened pig being sold to a butcher. Finally, the deal was closed. I followed my new master away, thinking I was the luckiest man in Babylon.

"I liked my new home. Nana-naid, my master, taught me how to grind the barley in the stone bowl that stood in the courtyard, how to build a fire in the oven, and then how to grind very fine sesame flour for honey cakes. I had a couch in the shed where his grain was stored. Swasti, the enslaved housekeeper, fed me well and was pleased when I helped her with the heavy tasks. This was the chance I had been waiting for to make myself valuable to my master and, potentially, to find a way to freedom.

"I asked Nana-naid to show me how to knead the bread and to bake. He was happy with how willing I was, so he taught me how. Later, when my skills were improving, I asked him to show me how to make honey cakes, and soon I was doing all the baking. My master was glad to do less work, but Swasti shook her head in disapproval: 'No work to do is bad for anyone,' she declared.

"I felt it was time for me to think of a way to earn money to buy my freedom. Since the baking was finished at noon, I thought Nana-naid would approve if I found profitable employment for the afternoons. Then the thought came to me, why not bake more honey cakes and sell them to the hungry people on the streets?

"I presented my plan to Nana-naid this way: 'If I can use my afternoons after the baking is finished to earn more money for you, wouldn't it be fair for you to share the money I earn with me so that I can have money of my own to spend on my wants and needs?'

"'Fair enough, fair enough,' he admitted. When I told him of my plan to sell our honey cakes, he was pleased. 'Here is what we will do,' he suggested. Sell two for a copper, then half of the copper will be mine to

THE LUCKIEST MAN IN BABYLON

pay for the flour, honey, and wood to bake them. I will divide the half in half again, and I'll take half and you can keep half. I was pleased by his generous offer, and that I could keep one fourth of the profit.

"That night, I worked late to make a tray to display the cakes on. Nana-naid gave me some of his old clothes so that I would look professional, and Swasti helped me wash the clothes and repair them. The next day, I baked an extra supply of honey cakes. They looked brown and tempting on the tray as I walked along the street, loudly advertising what I was selling. At first, no one seemed interested, and I was discouraged. I kept on though, and later in the afternoon, as people got hungry, the cakes began to sell, and soon my tray was empty.

"Nana-naid was pleased with my success and gladly paid me my share. I was happy to have some money. Megiddo had been right when he said a master appreciated good work from his slaves. That night I was so excited over my success that I could hardly sleep and tried to figure how much I could earn in a year and how many years would be required to buy my freedom.

"As I went out with my tray of cakes every day, I soon found regular customers. One of these was your grandfather, Arad Gula. He was a rug merchant who traveled from one end of the city to the other, accompanied by a donkey loaded high with rugs and a slave to lead the donkey. He would buy two cakes for himself and two for his slave, always hanging around to talk with me while they ate them. Your grandfather said something to me one day that I will always remember. 'I like your cakes, boy, but I like how you sell them even better. Such a positive attitude will take you far in life.' I wish you could understand, Hadan Gula, what these words of encouragement could mean to a slave boy, lonely in a big city, struggling with all he had in him to find a way out of his humiliation.

"As the months went by, I continued to add copper to my purse, and it began to have a comforting weight on my belt. Work was proving to be my best friend, just as Megiddo had said. I was happy but Swasti was worried. 'Your master, I'm afraid he's spending too much time at the casinos,' she warned.

"I was so happy one day to run into my friend Megiddo on the street. He was leading three donkeys loaded with vegetables to the market. 'I am doing very well,' he said. 'My master appreciated my good work and made me a foreman. He trusts the marketing to me, and he's also sending for my family. Work is helping me recover from the trouble I got into. Someday it will help me to buy my freedom, so I can have a farm of my own once more.'

"Time went on, and Nana-naid was more and more anxious for me to return from selling each day. He would be waiting and would eagerly count and divide our money. He would also urge me to seek further markets and increase my sales. I often went outside the city gates to solicit the overseers of the slaves building the walls. I hated to return to the disturbing sights, but the overseers were liberal buyers. One day, I was surprised to see Zabado waiting in line to fill his basket with bricks. He was gaunt and hunched over, and his back was covered with welts and sores from the whips of the overseers. I felt sorry for him, so I handed him a cake, which he shoved into his mouth like a hungry animal. Seeing the greedy look in his eyes, I ran before he could grab my tray.

"'Why do you work so hard?' Arad Gula asked me one day. Almost the same question you asked me today, do you remember? I told him what Megiddo had said about work and how it was proving to be my best friend. With pride, I showed him my wallet full of copper and explained how I was saving them to buy my freedom.

"'When you are free, what will you do?' he inquired.

"'I intend to become a merchant.'

"At that, he confided in me something unexpected, 'I'll bet you didn't know that I am a slave like you. I am in a partnership with my master.'

"Stop," interrupted Hadan Gula. "I will not listen to lies tarnishing the memory of my grandfather. He was not a slave." His eyes blazed in anger.

Sharru Nada remained calm. "I respected him for rising above his misfortune and becoming a leading citizen of Damascus. Do you take after your grandfather? Are you brave enough to face true facts, or do you prefer to live under false illusions?"

Hadan Gula straightened in his saddle. In a voice deep with suppressed emotion, he replied, "My grandfather was beloved by all. His good deeds were countless. When the famine came, he used his gold to buy grain from Egypt, and his caravan brought it to Damascus and distributed it to the people so none would starve. Now you say he was just a despised slave in Babylon."

"If he had remained a slave in Babylon he might have been despised, but when he became a great man in Damascus, due to his own hard work, the gods forgave his misfortunes and honored him with their respect," Sharru Nada replied.

"After telling me that he was a slave," Sharru Nada continued, "he explained how anxious he had been to earn his freedom. Now that he had enough money, he was overwhelmed and didn't know what to do. He was no longer making good sales and afraid to leave the support of his master. I protested his indecision: 'Don't rely on your master any more. Get that feeling of being free again—act like a free man and succeed like one! Decide what you want to accomplish, and work will help you achieve it!' He went on his way saying he was glad I had shamed him for his cowardice.[2]

"One day, I went outside the gates again and was surprised to find a crowd gathering there. When I asked a person for an explanation, he replied: 'Haven't you heard? An escaped slave, who murdered one of the King's guards, has been brought to justice and will be whipped to death for his crime today. Even the King himself will be here.'

[2] Slave customs in ancient Babylon, though they may seem inconsistent to us, were strictly regulated by law. For example, a slave could own property of any kind, even other slaves upon which his master had no claim. Slaves intermarried freely with non-slaves. Children of free mothers were free. Most of the city merchants were slaves. Many of these were in partnership with their masters and wealthy in their own right.

"The crowd was so dense around the whipping post, I was afraid the rest of my honey cakes would get stolen. I climbed up the unfinished wall to see over the heads of the people. I was fortunate to have a view of King Nebuchadnezzar himself as he rode by in his golden chariot. I'd never seen such grandeur—clothes and accessories of gold cloth and velvet.

"I couldn't see the whipping, but I could hear the shrieks of the poor slave. I wondered how one so noble as our handsome King could stand to see such suffering, but when I saw he was laughing and joking with his nobles, I knew he was cruel and understood why such inhumane tasks were demanded of the slaves building the walls. After the slave was dead, his body was hung on a pole by a rope attached to his leg so everyone could see. As the crowd began to thin, I approached the slave. On his hairy chest, I saw a tattoo of two entwined snakes. It was the Pirate.

"The next time I saw Arad Gula, he was a changed man. He greeted me enthusiastically: 'The slave you knew is now a free man. There was magic in your words. Already my sales and my profits are increasing, and my wife is overjoyed. She was a free woman, the niece of my master, and she wants us to move to a far away city where no one will know I was once a slave. Our children will not be punished for their father's misfortune. Work has become my best friend; it has allowed me to recapture my confidence and skills.' I was so happy that I could repay him for the encouragement he gave me, even if just in a small way.

"One evening, Swasti came to me in distress: 'Your master is in trouble. I'm afraid for him. A few months ago, he lost a lot of money at the casino. He doesn't pay the farmer for his grain or honey anymore, and he doesn't pay back the moneylender; they are both angry and are threatening him.'

"'Why should we worry over his troubles? We aren't responsible for him,' I replied thoughtlessly.

"'Stupid kid, you don't understand. He gave the moneylender your title to secure a loan. Under the law, he can claim and sell you. I don't know what to do. He is a good master. Why, oh why, did this have to happen to him?'

"Swasti's fears were valid. While I was baking the next morning, the moneylender returned with a man he called Sasi. This man looked at me and said I would do. The moneylender didn't wait for my master to return and told Swasti to tell him he had taken me. With only the clothes on my back, and the purse of copper hanging safely from my belt, I was taken from the unfinished baking. I was whirled away from my deepest hopes just like a hurricane snatches the tree from the forest and throws it into the stormy sea. Again, a casino and beer had caused me disaster.

"Sasi was a blunt, gruff man. As he led me across the city, I told him about the good work I had been doing for Nana-naid and said I hoped to do good work for him as well. His reply offered no encouragement: 'I do not like this work. My master does not like it. The King has told him to send me to build a section of the Grand Canal. Master tells Sasi, "buy more slaves, work hard and finish quick," but I don't know how can anyone can finish such a big job "quick".'

"Picture a desert with no trees, just low shrubs and a sun burning with such fury that the water in our barrels became so hot we could barely drink it. Then picture rows of men, going down into the deep excavation and lugging heavy baskets of dirt up soft, dusty trails, from sunrise to sunset. Picture food, served in open troughs from which we fed ourselves like pigs. We had no tents, not even straw for beds. That was the situation in which I found myself. I buried my wallet in a marked spot, wondering if I could ever dig it up again.

"At first, I worked with good will, but as the months dragged on, I felt my spirit breaking. Then the heat fever took hold of my weary body. I lost my appetite and could barely eat any of my meat and vegetables. At night, I would toss and turn restlessly. In my misery, I wondered if Zabado was the one who had the best plan, to run away and keep his back from being broken at work. Then, I recalled my last sight of him and knew his plan was not good. I thought of the Pirate with his bitterness and wondered if it might be just as well to fight and kill. The memory of his bleeding body reminded me that his plan was also useless. Then I remembered my last sight of Megiddo. His hands were deeply calloused from hard work, but his heart was light and there was happiness on his face. His was the best plan.

"Yet, I was just as willing to work as Megiddo; he couldn't have worked harder than I did. Why didn't my work bring me happiness and success? Was it work that brought Megiddo happiness, or was happiness and success merely in the laps of the gods? Was I going to work the rest of my life without reaching my goals, without happiness and success? All of these questions ran through my mind, and I didn't have an answer—I was so confused.

"Several days later, when I thought I was at the end of my endurance and my questions were still unanswered, Sasi sent for me. A messenger came from my master to take me back to Babylon. I dug up my precious wallet, wrapped myself in the tattered remnants of my clothes, and was on my way.

"As we rode, the same thoughts of a hurricane throwing me here and there kept racing through my nervous brain. I seemed to be living the weird words of a chant from my native town of Harroun:

Attacking someone like a whirlwind,
Driving them like a storm,
Whose course no one can predict,
Whose destiny no one can foretell.

"Was I going to be punished? What new miseries and disappointments awaited me?

"When we rode to the courtyard of my master's house, imagine my surprise when I saw Arad Gula waiting for me. He helped me down and hugged me like a long lost brother.

"As we went our way, I would have followed him in the way a slave should follow his master, but he would not allow me. He put his arm around me, saying, 'I looked everywhere for you. When I had almost given up hope, I met Swasti who told me about the moneylender, who then directed me to your owner. He drove a hard bargain and made me pay an outrageous price, but you are worth it. Your philosophy and your motivation have been my inspiration to this new success.'

"'Megiddo's philosophy, not mine,' I interrupted.

"'Megiddo's and yours. Thank you both. We are going to Damascus, and I need you to be my partner. In one moment you will be a free man!' As he said this, he took out the clay tablet with my slave title on it. He raised it above his head and hurled it to break into a hundred pieces on the cobblestones. He stamped upon the fragments happily until they were dust.

"Tears of gratitude filled my eyes. I knew I was the luckiest man in Babylon. Work, as you can see in this story of the hardest time in my life, proved to be my best friend. My willingness to work enabled me to escape from being sold to the slave gangs on the walls. It also impressed your grandfather so much that he selected me to be his partner."

Then Hadan Gula questioned, "Was work my grandfather's secret key to getting gold?"

"It was the only key he had when I first knew him," Sharru Nada replied. "Your grandfather enjoyed working. The gods appreciated his efforts and rewarded him liberally."

"I'm beginning to understand," Hadan Gula was speaking thoughtfully. "Work attracted many friends who admired his industry and the success it brought. Work brought him the honors he enjoyed so much in Damascus. Work brought him all those things I approve of. And I thought work was only for slaves."

"Life is rich with many pleasures for us to enjoy," Sharru Nada commented. "Each has its place. I am glad that work is not reserved for slaves. If that were the case, I would be deprived of my greatest pleasure. I enjoy many things, but nothing takes the place of work."

Sharru Nada and Hadan Gula rode in the shadows of the towering walls up to the massive, bronze gates of Babylon. At their approach, the gate guards jumped to attention and respectfully saluted an honored citizen. With head held high, Sharru Nada led the long caravan through the gates and up the streets of the city.

"I have always hoped to be a man like my grandfather," Hadan Gula confided to him. "I never realized what kind of man he was, but you've shown me. Now that I understand, I admire him all the more and feel more determined to be like him. I'm afraid I can never repay you for giving me the true key to his success. From this day forth, I will use his key. I will start humbly, as he started, which befits me far better than jewels and fine robes."

As he said this, Hadan Gula pulled the jewels from his ears and the rings from his fingers. Then, reining in his horse, he dropped back and rode with deep respect behind the leader of the caravan.

Afterword – A Historical Sketch of Babylon

A note for the Modern Language Edition – Since the original publication of this book in 1926, more about the history of Babylon has been discovered. Many of the facts below have been proven incorrect.

In the pages of history, there lives no city more glamorous than Babylon. Its very name conjures visions of wealth and splendor. Its treasures of gold and jewels were fabulous. One naturally pictures such a wealthy city located in a suitable setting of tropical luxury, surrounded by rich, natural resources of forests, and mines—such was not the case for Babylon. It was located beside the Euphrates River, in a flat, arid valley. It had no forests, mines, or stones for building. It was not even located on a natural trade route, and the rainfall was insufficient to raise crops.

Babylon is an outstanding example of humanity's ability to achieve great objectives, using whatever means available. All of the resources supporting this large city were man-made.

Babylon possessed just two natural resources—fertile soil and water in the river. With one of the greatest engineering accomplishments of this or any other day, Babylonian engineers diverted the waters from the river by means of dams and immense irrigation canals. Far out across that arid valley went these canals to pour the life giving waters over the fertile soil. This ranks among the first engineering feats known to history. Abundant crops were the reward of this irrigation system the world had never seen before.

Fortunately, during its long existence, Babylon was ruled by successive lines of kings to whom conquest and devastation were but incidental.

While it engaged in many wars, most of these were local or defensive against ambitious conquerors from other countries who wanted the fabulous treasures of Babylon. The outstanding rulers of Babylon live on in history because of their wisdom, enterprise, and justice. Babylon did not produce any arrogant royals seeking to conquer the known world so that all nations would praise their conceitedness.

As a city, Babylon does not exist anymore. When those energizing human forces that built and maintained the city for thousands of years were withdrawn, it soon became a deserted ruin. The site of the city is in Asia, about six hundred miles east of the Suez Canal, just north of the Persian Gulf. The latitude is about thirty degrees above the equator, approximately the same as that of Yuma, Arizona. It possessed a climate similar to that of this American city, hot and dry.

Today, this valley of the Euphrates, once a populous, irrigated farming district, is again a windswept, arid wasteland. Limited grass and desert shrubs strive for existence against the windblown sands. Gone are the fertile fields, the massive cities, and the long caravans of rich merchandise. Nomadic bands, earning a very modest living by tending small herds, are the only inhabitants. It has been this way since about the beginning of the Christian era.

Dotting this valley are earthen hills. For centuries, they were considered by travelers to be nothing else. The attention of archeologists was finally attracted to them because of broken pieces of pottery and brick that were washed down by the occasional rain storms. Expeditions, financed by European and American museums, were sent here to excavate and see what could be found. Picks and shovels soon proved these hills to be ancient cities. City graves, they might well be called. Babylon was one of these—over the course of twenty centuries the winds had scattered the desert dust. Built originally of brick, all exposed walls had disintegrated and gone back to earth once more. Such is Babylon, the wealthy city, today; a heap of dirt, so long abandoned that no living person even knew its name until it was discovered by carefully removing the refuse of centuries from the streets and the fallen wreckage of its noble temples and palaces.

Many scientists consider the civilization of Babylon, and other cities in this valley, to be the oldest of which there is a definite record. Positive dates have been proved reaching back 8000 years. An interesting fact in this connection is the means used to determine these dates. Uncovered in the ruins of Babylon were descriptions of an eclipse of the sun. Modern astronomers readily computed the time when such an eclipse, visible in Babylon, occurred and thus established a known relationship between their calendar and our own. In this way, we have proved that 8000 years ago, the Sumerites, who inhabited Babylonia, were living in walled cities. One can only guess how many centuries these cities existed. Their inhabitants were not mere barbarians living within protective walls; they were an educated and enlightened people. So far as written history goes, they were the first engineers, astronomers, mathematicians, financiers, and the first people to have a written language.

Mention has already been made of the irrigation systems, which transformed the arid valley into an agricultural paradise. The remains of these canals can still be traced, although they are mostly filled with accumulated sand. Some of them were of such size that, when empty of water, a dozen horses could be ridden side by side along their bottoms. In size, they compare favorably with the largest canals in Colorado and Utah. In addition to irrigating the valley lands, Babylonian engineers completed another project of similar magnitude. By means of an elaborate drainage system, they reclaimed an immense area of swamp land at the mouths of the Euphrates and Tigris Rivers and began growing crops there.

Herodotus, the Greek traveler and historian, visited Babylon while it was in its prime and has given us the only known description by an outsider. His writings give a graphic description of the city and some of the unusual customs of its people. He mentions the remarkable fertility of the soil and the bountiful harvest of wheat and barley they produced.

The glory of Babylon has faded, but its wisdom has been preserved for us. For this, we are indebted to their form of records. In that distant day, the use of paper had not been invented. Instead, they laboriously engraved their writing on tablets of moist clay. When completed, these were baked and became hard tiles. They were about six by eight inches, and an inch thick. These clay tablets, as they are commonly called, were used as often as we use modern forms of writing. Upon them were engraved legends, poetry, history, transcriptions of royal decrees, the laws of the land, titles to property, promissory notes, and even letters, which were dispatched by messengers to distant cities. From these clay tablets we are permitted an insight into the intimate, personal affairs of the people. For example, one tablet, evidently from the records of a country storekeeper, relates that on the given date a certain customer brought in a cow and exchanged it for seven sacks of wheat, three being delivered immediately, and the other four to await the customer's request. Safely buried in the wrecked cities, archeologists have recovered entire libraries of these tablets, hundreds of thousands of them.

One of the outstanding wonders of Babylon was the immense walls surrounding the city. The ancients ranked them with the great pyramid of Egypt as belonging to the seven wonders of the world. Queen Semiramis is credited with having erected the first walls during the early history of the city. Modern excavations have been unable to find any trace of the original walls, nor is their exact height known, however, from mention made by early writers, it is estimated they were about fifty to sixty feet high, faced on the outer side with burnt brick, and further protected by a deep moat of water.

The later and more famous walls were started about six hundred years before the time of Christ by King Nabopolassar. He planned the rebuilding on such a gigantic scale that he did not live to see the work finished. This was left to his son, Nebuchadnezzar II, whose name is familiar in Biblical history. The height and length of these later walls staggers belief. They are reported upon reliable authority to have been about one hundred and sixty feet high, the equivalent of the height of a modern fifteen story office building. The total length is estimated to be between nine and eleven miles. The top was so wide that a six-horse chariot could be driven around them. Of this tremendous structure, little now remains except portions of the foundations and the moat. In addition to the ravages of the elements, others in the region throughout the centuries completed the destruction by quarrying the brick for building purposes elsewhere.

Against the walls of Babylon marched, in turn, the victorious armies of almost every conqueror of that age of wars of conquest. A host of kings laid siege to Babylon, but always in vain. Invading armies of that day were not to be considered lightly. Historians speak of such units as 10,000 horsemen, 25,000 chariots, 1,200 regiments of foot soldiers with 1,000 soldiers to the unit. Often two or three years of preparation would be required to assemble war materials and depots of food along the proposed line of march. The city of Babylon was organized much like a modern city with streets and shops. Peddlers offered their wares through residential districts. Priests officiated in magnificent temples. Within the city was an inner enclosure for the royal palaces. The walls around this were said to have been higher than those surrounding the city.

The Babylonians were skilled in the arts, including sculpture, painting, weaving, gold working, and the manufacture of metal weapons and agricultural implements. Their jewelers created the most artistic jewelry. Many samples have been recovered from the graves of its wealthy citizens and are now on exhibition in the leading museums of the world.

At a very early period when the rest of the world was still hacking at trees with stone-headed axes, or hunting and fighting with flint-pointed spears and arrows, the Babylonians were using axes, spears, and arrows with metal heads. The Babylonians were clever financiers and traders. So far as we know, they were the original inventors of money as a means of exchange, of promissory notes, and written titles to property.

Babylon was never entered by hostile armies until about 540 years before the birth of Christ, but even then the walls were not captured.

113

The story of the fall of Babylon is unusual; Cyrus, one of the great conquerors of that period, intended to attack the city and hoped to take its impregnable walls. Advisors of Nabonidus, the King of Babylon, persuaded him to go meet Cyrus and give him battle without waiting for the city to be invaded. In the succeeding defeat to the Babylonian army, it fled away from the city. Cyrus, thereupon, entered the open gates and took possession without resistance. Thereafter, the power and prestige of the city gradually waned until, in the course of a few hundred years, it was eventually abandoned, deserted, left for the winds and storms to level once again to that desert earth from which its grandeur had originally been built. Babylon had fallen, never to rise again, but to it civilization owes much.

The eons of time have crumbled to dust the proud walls of its temples, but the wisdom of Babylon endures.

Money is the medium by which earthly success is measured.

Money makes possible the enjoyment of the best the earth affords.

Money is plentiful for those who understand the simple laws that govern its acquisition.

Today, money is governed by the same laws that controlled it when prosperous people thronged the streets of Babylon, thousands of years ago.

Printed in Great Britain
by Amazon